HOMER

is Where the Heart Is

JOHN RANDALL TABOR

iUniverse, Inc.
Bloomington

Homer is Where the Heart Is

iUniverse books may be ordered through booksellers or by contacting:

iUniverse
1663 Liberty Drive
Bloomington, IN 47403
www.iuniverse.com
1-800-Authors (1-800-288-4677)

Because of the dynamic nature of the Internet, any web addresses or links contained in this book may have changed since publication and may no longer be valid. The views expressed in this work are solely those of the author and do not necessarily reflect the views of the publisher, and the publisher hereby disclaims any responsibility for them.

Any people depicted in stock imagery provided by Thinkstock are models, and such images are being used for illustrative purposes only.

Certain stock imagery © Thinkstock.

ISBN: 978-1-4620-3159-7 (sc)
ISBN: 978-1-4620-3160-3 (e)

Printed in the United States of America

iUniverse rev. date: 07/20/2011

Acknowledgment

To my son, Jonathan Calman Tabor, for his help and support in formatting and transmitting the manuscript and graphics of this book to the editors at iUniverse.

Dedication

This book is dedicated to my father, C.L. Tabor, Jr., who died on February, 10, 2003, and to the people, past and present, of Homer, Louisiana. They made this book a reality.

Author Notation

An asterisk next to a name indicates the use of a pseudonym for that person. In every case, the person is real, as well as the actions and events connected to him.

Introduction

When my Homer High School fiftieth reunion was held in 2008 I was asked to list all the towns and cities where I had lived. Although those abodes took me to all parts of the state of Louisiana none held my heart like my birthplace, Homer. Through the years I moved from Homer to places like Ruston (Louisiana Tech), Baton Rouge (Louisiana State University), and Shreveport (LSU in Shreveport), but I kept coming back home to Homer where an integral part of my soul remains.

Although I have not had a home in Homer since 1998 I live there still through a mixture of kaleidoscopical memories. They are like old friends. Some produce a smile, a few cause unabashed laughter, fewer still bring a bit of sadness. The memories are bittersweet, sometimes painful, but even these are a part of the whole Homer picture. If perchance we never felt pain, remorse or despair then our brief stay here would be less than a full life, and appreciation for the good would suffer. Thus, the memories in the following pages are not always idyllic, but whatever they happen to be on any given page—good, bad or somewhere between—as I grow older they fill me more and more with their splendor and create a longing to go back in time and relive those days, see again all those flawed, wonderful people in Homer, where together we might re-create and re-experience our various heartbreaks, joys, triumphs, disappointments, laughters, and loves.

In Wallace Stegner's 1977 National Book Award winner, *The Spectator Bird*, the protagonist Joe Allston muses, "...it is one thing to examine your life and quite another to write it. Writing your life implies that you think it worth writing. It implies an arrogance, or confidence, or compulsion to justify oneself, that I can't claim. Did Washington write his memoirs? Did Lincoln, Jefferson, Shakespeare, Socrates? No."

However, narrating the events of our lives is a part of the human condition. We do this to not only communicate with other people, but also to make sense of our own lives. *Homer Is Where the Heart Is* is not only my attempt at accomplishing those tasks, it is a humble legacy that I wish to share with my children and grandchildren so that they can more fully know and understand their father/grandfather and the conditions and culture that surrounded his life. That is the primary purpose of this book.

Part I of this book recounts pieces of a life growing up in a small town of approximately four to five thousand. Part II moves into the adult phase and includes in various forms a number of newspaper columns that I did for *The* (Homer, Louisiana) *Guardian-Journal* from 2002-2003. These columns spawned the germ of *Homer Is Where the Heart Is.* The columns not only focus on Homerites, but also my family members, and friends, and colleagues at Louisiana State University in Shreveport, where I was a faculty/staff member from 1968-2001. When I received so much positive feedback from readers of those columns I began to consider using those writings as a springboard into what turned out to be this book.

Part 1

> *Whatsoever things are true, whatsoever things are honest, whatsoever things are just, whatsoever things are pure, whatsoever things are lovely, whatsoever things are of good report; if there be any virtue, and if there be any praise, think on these things.*
>
> Philippians 4:8

Early Memories

Normally the onset of autobiographical memories begins at the age of three or four, but my earliest memory seems to pre-date that. Legitimate or not, the memory is of me lying on my back in the middle of one of the many bedrooms in my grandparents' house on what used to be Pine Street (now called East Fifth). The bed was surrounded on the sides and the foot by an admiring group of adults who must have been grandparents, parents, aunts, and uncles.

My parents lived in Granddaddy and Grandma Tabor's home and, from time to time, my three uncles and one aunt did also. For awhile this room of memory was where my parents, my brother, and I slept, in a house where we celebrated at least one Christmas. My memory of that occasion is a tin mechanical train racing around circular tracks, shooting out sparks at the hemline of my mother's Christmas housecoat. I imagined her going up in flames.

For another while we slept in the one room upstairs. A solid, wooden, two-tier staircase, the strongest part of the house, led us up there each night at bedtime, and during our ascent Daddy followed behind me, speeding me along with playful pinches to my buttocks, saying, "Fleas are biting. Fleas are biting." The pinches were so subtle that at first I thought fleas had vacated my mutt Shorty and decided to ride up the stairs on my backside. Later, I knew it was Daddy and this was his way of showing that he loved me.

Every morning I awoke all alone in that remote, forsaken room and felt an acute sense of abandonment. Immediately I bounced out of bed and, with a quick, agile turn at the landing, raced into the warm kitchen where the sweet aroma of baking biscuits and fresh coffee enveloped the room. There I felt safe with my mother, my grandmother, and my Aunt Marguerite, who made a ritual of placing me on her lap, and with a comforting smile, and laughter in her brown eyes, singing to me: *"Ha! Ha! Ha! You and me. Little brown jug I do love thee…"*

The only person who called me John rather than Randall when I was a child, was Granddaddy Tabor. He never called me Randall like everyone else did. Maybe it was because his father was a John, John Burl Tabor, my great grandfather.

We felt at home with nicknames. Granddaddy was called "Chuck" by his sons, my dad was either "Red" or "Son," Uncle Maurice was better known as "Dude," Uncle Hutto was either "Hut" or "Pluto," and I was "Little Buddy."

In the 1940s, just before my father, C.L. Tabor, Jr., was drafted into the U.S. Army the family moved from Homer to Columbia, La. where Dad worked in oilfields. What I remember most from that town is my dad's roughneck buddies, cooling down under the sparse shade of pine trees, sipping from large bottles of RC cola, calling me by the name "Smokey," and roaring with a chorus of contagious laughter at my inability to pronounce "Columbia." It came out something like "Conumerra" or "Combunia." Years later I realized that my butchering that word and many others as well was very much linked to my lifetime hearing loss, which I shall discuss in greater detail later.

World War II was a part of my early life even if I didn't fully understand it. The name *Hitler* seemed to resonate daily throughout the house, where Hitler actually came to life at times, portrayed by Uncle Hutto , who marched from room to room, a small black comb squeezed between his nose and upper lip, his black hair brushed down to his right eye, giving everyone a Nazi salute and bellowing, "Heil, Hitler." But to my deficient ears it sounded like "Hell Hitler." In this dictator role, Hutto amused himself by stuffing me inside a dark closet next to the fireplace, shutting the closet door and ignoring for a while my pleas to be released. It wasn't a concentration camp, but, still, it was pretty scary.

Hitler's war reached into the Tabor household and took Hutto's brothers one by one: first Uncle Elton, who served in the jungles of New Guinea, then Uncle Dude, who left us in 1944, and finally Daddy, despite the fact that he had a wife and two children.

Before Daddy was drafted, the family bundled up with blankets on a cold night and made the long drive to Montgomery, Alabama, to bring home my Uncle Elton. The little coupe was packed with Momma, Grandma, Aunt

Marguerite, me, and Daddy, who drove. I remember little of the return home except that it was still cold and it must have been around Christmas time. Back in Homer whenever Elton tried to sleep during the day, Alton Ray James, a kid who lived next door, started popping holiday fireworks. The series of explosions startled Elton awake, and for a moment he seemed to be back in the jungles of New Guinea. This reaction was frightening to me and I hoped that Daddy would not leave me as Uncle Elton had, snatched away to the distant Gulf of Papua.

When Uncle Dude came home from Europe, carrying himself with a confident swagger, I saw a true conquering hero. On the floor in the middle of my grandparents' living room he dropped a bulging olive green Santa-like canvas bag filled with presents for everyone, even me. My gift was a book, bound in red, filled with the cartoon misfortunes of Sad Sack as a G.I. in the U.S. Army. It is a treasure, and I still have it, sans front cover.

When Daddy was drafted,that old feeling of abandonment returned. My mother, brother and I lived with relatives in three places: Homer, Shreveport, Arcadia, then back to Homer. My father attempted to console his mother in a letter that follows (abbreviated):

Dearest Folks,

How are you doing? I am fine but never will learn to like it.

Don't forget what I told you about Hut. If he can't keep his size down he had better slow his age down or he might learn how Army life is.

Mother, have you ever stopped crying yet? You know that won't help matters any at all. You should really be proud you have had three sons serving in Uncle Sam's Army. That means plenty. Think of Mrs. Noland.

So one day this mess is all going to be over and everybody will be so happy.

Do you have any roomers yet? You might as well get some money for you never know how long this will last.

Keep your chin up now for worry only makes you grow old quicker.

Tell Hut he should be making some good money somewhere and I don't mean just a little. He is big enough to roughneck.

Lots of love,
Pvt. Tabor

Approximately one year later Momma received a more uplifting letter from the U.S. War Department:

gjr/4103

WAR DEPARTMENT
THE ADJUTANT GENERAL'S OFFICE
WASHINGTON 25, D.C.

IN REPLY REFER TO:
AGPE-A 201 Tabor, Charles L.
(25 Apr 46)

17 JUN 1946

Mrs. Gracie K. Tabor
Box 23
Arcadia, Louisana

Dear Mrs. Tabor:

I have your letter relative to the discharge of the above named soldier from military service.

War Department records indicate that this enlisted man has been discharged from military service. You are, no doubt, enjoying a happy reunion with him.

I am exceedingly sorry that I was unable to furnish you with this information at an earlier date.

Sincerely yours,

EDWARD F. WITSELL
Major General
The Adjutant General

gjr/4103

WAR DEPARTMENT

IN REPLY REFER TO:
AGPE-A 201 Tabor, Charles L.

(25 Apr 46)

THE ADJUTANT GENERAL'S OFFICE
WASHINGTON, 25, D.C.

Mrs. Gracie K. Tabor
Box 23
Arcadia, Louisana (sic)

Dear Mrs. Tabor:

I have your letter relative to the discharge of the above named soldier from military service.

War Department records indicate that this enlisted man has been discharged from military service. You are, no doubt, enjoying a happy reunion with him.

I am exceedingly sorry that I was unable to furnish you with This information at an earlier date.

Sincerely yours,

EDWARD F. WITSELL
Major General
The Adjutant General

After Daddy was released from the Army in 1946 we came to reside in Bossier City, across the Red River from Shreveport. We lived in a cramped house trailer a fraction of the size of those today, and where I listened on the radio as Joe Louis retained the heavyweight championship of the world, and he quickly became my boxing hero until a score of visiting adults informed me that Joe was a Negro and that I would probably want to pick somebody else. Thus, I sat at the dining table, which folded into the wall when we weren't eating, and ate my tutti-frutti ice cream and tried to understand racism.

Although my mother remains in denial about this, during warm spring and summer months living in that trailer I averaged at least one switching on my bare legs each day. I have no idea what I was doing to stay on Momma's bad side. My guess is that I could not hear her call out to me from the steps of the trailer to quit playing and to come home. When I became a father in 1969 and 1970 I punished my children, too, but I never used a switch. I saw it as an instrument of torture.

I remember the town of Homer in the forties and fifties draped in sleepy sepia tones of brown and gray, offering its visitors via a sign across the street from the First Baptist Church the simple aphorism, *Make Homer Your Home.* My young mind was convinced that no rational being could possibly reject such an invitation. It was not just any town. It was one whose businesses were laid out in a perfect square, with its crown jewel standing majestically in the center: a two-story antebellum parish courthouse of Greek Revival architecture. Built in 1861 for $12,000, it is the only antebellum courthouse in the state that still serves its original purpose. There has never been a time in my life when I have not been in awe of it.

Hot Tamale Charlie

After we moved into our first real house at 401 Keener Street, one of the best things in Homer during the early years was the Saturday night appearances of Hot Tamale Charlie, a Mexican vendor who towed his wooden cart full of steaming, corn-shucked tamales from El Dorado, Arkansas, and set up shop on the Square. Charlie's ringing voice could be heard from any section of the Square, even by those hard of hearing: "Hot tamales! Get your hot tamales right here! Hot tamales! It's Hot Tamale Charlie! Hot tamales!" And if you listened carefully you heard an occasional, "And that ain't all." In my childhood naivete I believed that Charlie could make a decent living peddling his goods for basically eight cents a tamale. The fact that Homer was dry fit nicely into Charlie's entrepreneurial plans.

Saturday nights were special in Homer. First it might be a supper of fried oysters at the Majestic Café, followed by Abbott and Costello at the Pelican Theater. The moment we left the theater, we would hear Charlie's cry and track it down. Then Daddy, for one dollar, would purchase four groups of three tamales, bound with string and wrapped in newspapers, and then drive us home as quickly as possible while the tamales were still "good 'n hot." Once there we headed to the back of the house where the large kitchen was, unwrapped the newspaper, put down some plates and forks and dug in. Hot tamale heaven.

Cho Chos

Across North Second Street from Homer's ice plant, the two-story wooden Claiborne Creamery sat in the 1940s offering a unique and popular ice-cream treat on a stick called the Cho Cho. An extremely delicious concoction with a subtle chocolate malt flavor, it sold for five cents. It came in a cardboard container about the size of a Dixie cup.

First, you had to roll it between your hands to soften the ice cream, then you pressed it out the bottom of the cup, and then you were at the best step of all, eating it. At the time, I thought the Cho Cho was made exclusively by the local creamery, but I now know Cho Chos were available across the country. Everybody talks about how good they were, using words like *tasty, dreamy, comforting, delicious, cooling, nourishing.* Getting a Cho Cho on a hot summer day was *all* of the above. My question is this: if they were so good why in tarnation did they stop making something so popular?

A little research provides some interesting facts. The Carnation Company introduced the Cho Cho on June 6, 1939, but the trademark was reassigned to the Popsicle Company in 1982; then in 2003, the brand/product expired. Today you can get a Cho Cho at Tucker's Ice Cream Parlor in Alameda, California, if you're willing to go that distance. I've heard that some people are planning their next vacation to the west coast so that they can re-live their childhood ice-cream treat. It won't be a nickel anymore, and it may not be the same thing that we loved in the 1940s.

Because I was not willing to drive 2,000 miles to find out, I tried to re-create the Cho Cho in the kitchen of my home. I mixed some Carnation

Chocolate Malt with some vanilla ice cream and milk, then put it in the freezer. An hour or two later I dug into this mixture. At first bite, I said aloud to this concoction, "You're pretty good, but you're no Cho Cho." It was a failure.

Maybe I will drive those 2,000 miles.

Early Activities

Halloween and Christmas back in those days were special. It was 1946 or 1947 the Christmas Eve that Uncle Dude nodded toward a wrapped box the size of an elephant and said, "That's yours," meaning that whatever was inside would belong to me as soon as I tore the paper off, an action timed at slightly less than the movement of light.

However, once the wrapping was off, a smaller box greeted me. And inside that box was still another box. Once I had gone through about three boxes of decreasing size, I concluded with dismay that whatever lay in the last box would not be enthusiastically received. As the boxes grew smaller, I sighed and muttered, "Socks. That's what it is. A pair of socks." I was sure of it.

Finally, after opening about five boxes within boxes, I came to the gift itself: pure gold, as in matching pairs of golden boxing gloves. Uncle Dude wasted no time in lacing me up and sparing with me, and coaching me in the fundamentals that I so admired in Joe Palooka and Curly Kayo.

Through the years those gloves were put to frequent use as we neighborhood kids staged our own Madison Square Garden events. Contenders were Jerry Tarpley, Herbie Whitman, Craig Hogan, Kenneth and Johnny Gordon, and a couple of Yankee kids who had just moved to Homer. We especially wanted to whip those Yankee brothers for no other reason than they were from north of Mason-Dixon. Managed expertly by Marion Henry White, our teenage neighbor who was older than the rest of us, we did just that, proudly preserving our Southern Heritage. Marion Henry's genius centered around his demands that our water intake between rounds not be swallowed, but only swished and expelled. I lost a couple of already loose teeth in these battles. This was considerably more fun than tying a string from my tooth to a doorknob and then slamming the door. That's how we pulled teeth in those days.

Santa was as good as Uncle Dude that year, bringing me a wagon of solid wood. I loved my wagon so much that it got equal time with the gloves. In fact the gloves often stayed on while the wagon was pulled.

Eventually I got the lowdown on Saint Nick and celebrated Christmas a little early by discovering "Santa" in our attic ten days before December 25. I was smart about my discovery, pretending innocence and keeping the Christmas gravy train flowing for Christmases to come. I could not just allow those toys to lie undisturbed for the eternity of ten days. So, whenever Mom and Dad took off to visit out-of-town relatives, out came a kitchen chair to give me the needed boost to ascend into the attic. Out came toy pistols and holsters and little cars and trucks and farm animals and magic kits and chemistry sets, pinball machines, toy cash registers, toy typewriters......

Then after an allotment of time back they went into the attic, as if they had never been moved. Somehow that Christmas was not the same, not as special. It marked the end of Christmas innocence.

One of the best things we did in Homer during the Christmas seasons of the 1940s and early 1950s was seeing the Christmas lights around town. Before television came to Homer, the family would hop into the 1946 Chevrolet and motor around just looking at people's lights. Night after night. The same lights over and over. They were that good. But no decorative touch matched the center of town, where a rainbow of lights strung from the top of the courthouse to the business buildings across the streets turned the Square into a breathtaking, mountainous carousel. And Santa made an annual appearance atop the Coca-Cola Bottling Company along with his sleigh and reindeer. It was the epitome of Christmas, and it never got anywhere near boring.

Though I remember the boxing gloves and wagons and toys in the attic and even the licorice candy and socks from Grandma, what I really treasure are those drives around Homer to see the lights, along with newly cut cedar trees, the sounds of carolers, the bustling activity of last-minute shoppers around the Square. Long after material gifts have decayed and disappeared, yuletide memories will survive the years.

Halloween

Uncle Dude went all out for Halloween as well. His plentiful supply of candies and goodies was ample to satisfy the young appetites of the hoard of trick-or-treaters who showed up at his house. A smart guy, he long ago learned the Halloween secret to protecting his home against the pranks of tricksters, while at the same time topping the Best Customer List at Piggly Wiggly and Jitney Jungle. He even kept statistics. He counted the visitors. After I wrote an article for *The Guardian-Journal* in 2002 about his Halloween generosity, the number of callers increased from 362 to 466. The next year the number fell back to 412.

Halloween was always special to me, too. Guess it's in the genes. In the early years it was trick-or-treating in the old neighborhood or hosting a backyard party complete with a witch's heavy, black caldron. I was the witch with apple boobs swelling beneath my black dress, and wondered why my mother was laughing at my costume. I only wanted to be a realistic witch.

As I moved up to the young teen status, the trick-or-treating expanded to all parts of Homer. During that era we didn't worry about poison apples and razor blades, just whether or not our benefactors would slip an orange or banana into our bags rather than a package of peanut butter and molasses Kits.

On one particular Halloween night during my early teens a few buddies and I knocked on the front door of a house just off the north side of the Square. When the door creaked open, we sang in unison, "Trick or treat!" and opened our paper sacks expectedly. A little old lady peered at us and mumbled, "Oh, I didn't know it was Halloween."

You are kidding! How can anyone not know it's Halloween! Is this for real?

There was only one possible answer to this conundrum. This woman had to be a *communiss*. Yeah, that was it. She was a *communiss*.

Years later, as a student at Louisiana Tech, I took a required class called "Democracy versus Communism." Halfway through the course I came to realize that the poor little lady who upset us years ago with her Halloween ignorance was in fact not a communist and probably never was.

Outside

When I was a kid, we MADE things. First, we didn't have the money to buy them. Second, we felt within ourselves an unbridled sense of creativity, which we put to good use. Empty Coke bottles and blocks of wood became little cars that were driven on the roads of the crawl-space underworld beneath our house, which sat supported on concrete cinder blocks. Under the house is where we spent each summer day constructing roads on the dry, sandy terrain of the low east side and the marsh-like damp side of the upper west side. Where I "lived," the slanting rays of the outside real sun provided an almost resort-like atmosphere. It was like the differences between north and south Louisiana, except that this was one town.

I ran the east side, where I had my home, my cars, and my business. It was always some type of successful show business, a circus, a house of magic, a carnival. On the down side, too many times in my enthusiasm for the world of make believe, I hit the ol' noggin on either zigzagging water pipes or the actual floor of the real house, which I pretended was the sky above this mythical village. For those on the west side, it was even more dangerous. The bottom of the real house was lower to the ground there and the house slanted from the real living room and Mom and Dad's bedroom, down to the real kitchen on the east end.

Up on the west side, the cattle industry flourished, with cardboard cutouts of *Progressive Farmer* Jerseys, Brahmans, Holsteins, and Black Anguses. Thus, the farmers lived up west and the entrepreneurs stayed down east. Cultural differences even in the world of make-believe.

When we were not under the house we were outside climbing sycamore trees, building things like high-jumping pits, forts, tree houses, and discovering hiding places. The best thing was the cable ride that we erected between two backyard trees. We achieved this feat by attaching a rope and pulley to a wire cable that we stretched between a sycamore and a sweet gum tree, just above their largest branches. To start the ride, that went from tree to tree, we grabbed the rope attached to the pulley with both hands and then shoved ourselves from the large branch of the first tree and then glided somewhat rapidly to the other tree. It was a lengthy ride and quite exhilarating.

Sometimes during the construction phase of this project, I took some falls onto the sweet gum balls strewn plentifully on the ground below our work site. In retrospect, these occasional falls could very well explain a few things about me.

Elementary School

Our academic guidance in the early years was in the hands of teams of two lady teachers per grade in the old Homer Grammar School building that stretched stories above us like a dark, gothic castle. In the first grade we were divided equally between Mrs. Cady and Mrs. Whitlow. I had carried into Mrs. Whitlow's room on the first floor a deep phobia and distrust of doctors and nurses. During the first week of our classes Mrs. Whitlow informed us that we would be marching from her room in single file to a place she called the auditorium. Alas, this mysterious destination was not in my young, but developing, word bank. My panicky emotions convinced my mind that something medical, like the aforementioned doctors and nurses, and maybe even *shots*, was connected with this auditorium place.

Mrs. Whitlow, for reasons known only to her, chose me to lead us there, but at the moment of departure, I balked. And nothing she said could change my mind. I was not going to move from my frozen spot for anyone or anything, not for a package of peanut butter and molasses Kits, not even for a Cho Cho from the Claiborne Creamery.

Mrs. Whitlow viewed my resistant behavior as insubordination, and right away she provided me my first school spanking. Then when she picked a girl as my replacement, my humiliation was almost as great as my fear. Moments later, buffered by braver classmates, I saw an auditorium for the first time. To my relief, there were no tables stocked with bottles of rubbing alcohol, no balls of white cotton, and no nurses sitting at those tables holding a syringe in each hand. My phobia melted away and I was no longer afraid of *auditorium*, but I was never again asked to lead the class anywhere.

I have concluded that I am self-destructive. One day Mrs. Whitlow gave us a little test of ten very simple questions. We answered them by placing a check mark next to the word *yes* or the word *no*. I was breezing through the quiz with no trouble until I got to #8. The question was "Can a house run?" I was so outraged that such a silly, mindless question would be offered to us that I purposefully, in a sort of protest, I suppose, checked *yes*. Instead of making a perfect score, I got a nine, a B instead of an A. How dare "they" ask such a question. Did "they" believe we were kindergarteners?

We ate our school lunches in a dark cellar-like, windowless room that seemed like a dungeon dug deep into the bowels of the earth. Most of us brought from our homes stained brown paper bags, wrinkled from overuse and filled with tuna fish sandwiches, apples, and maybe a small piece of candy for dessert. It was a noisy place, with a lot of talking, joking, punching, and laughing. When the clamor reached a certain level, our principal, Mr. Tanner, would start flickering the lights to get us to pipe down. When he did that, the tone dropped to an Italian ritardando only to rest like a Generalpause and then build into an even louder fortissimo. Then the cycle would repeat. There was never a day that the lights were not flickered.

In the fall of 1949 we students moved to a new school building about a mile away, a one-story sprawling "chicken coop" as my Grandfather Tabor called it. Here, we had the option of walking like a caterpillar in a long line of pairs curving to the nearby high school cafeteria or eating our sack lunches in our new school's fresh, airy lunchroom.

It was in this room early one afternoon in the spring of 1950 that Mr. Tanner called a meeting with sixth and seventh grade boys. It must be something big, I thought. Just the top two grades and just boys invited. I was in the sixth grade so I was there with all the other guys.

Mr. Tanner, a large, gentle man with eyeglasses so thick that you could not see his eyes with clarity, stood tall before us and asked, "How many of you know what this means?"

Then he gave us the finger.

His towering right arm seemed like the trail of an ascending rocket ship, lingering and lingering, stopping time, the long, bony finger staring down at us like a fixed face of Mount Rushmore. It seemed to hang forever above his head, with no intention of ever coming down, but with the idea of keeping our collective, mesmerized pupils staring up, our youthful necks turned back, our chins jutting out. In that brief moment of time, which seemed endless, I came to realize that the old boundaries between my young world of being a child and that world of adulthood that Mr. Tanner lived in, were slowly evaporating, being erased forever. From this point on I would no longer be a child.

Hypnotized by that appendage, I looked at no one else. And no one uttered a sound until Mr. Tanner finally spoke again. "A few of our girls have said that some sixth and seventh grade boys have made this sign at them. If any of you here have done this, made this sign to girls, I want it to stop immediately."

Then our silence was broken, when from the back of the room, my former firecracker-loving neighbor, seventh-grader Alton Ray James, who had already been held back several grades, responded in a deep, slow-moving voice, "Mr. Tanner, what if a girl gives it to you?"

"Alton, have any girls made this sign to you?"

Then, as if he needed a moment to think, Alton said in his slow manner, "High school girls."

Mr. Tanner retired at the end of the 1956–57 school year. By that time Alton Ray was an inmate at Angola State Penitentiary.

Early Jobs

The Shreveport Journal

Most of the time I had part-time jobs in the forties, fifties, and sixties. One of the first was selling the *Shreveport Journal* afternoon newspaper on the streets of Homer, usually in the vicinity of the Square. Each afternoon after school I received an allotment of about thirty copies of the *Journal* at Schultz's newsstand, put them under an arm and got to work. At first I barked out so that people on the town sidewalks knew that I had a good, reasonably priced product to sell at five cents. But, before very long, I didn't have to say a word. They knew that I was the *Journal* representative and that I would be there to serve them each and every day without fail.

In the beginning I shared this responsibility with Bill James, the younger brother of Alton Ray James. A few years back those two had spent a single night in the Homer jail for stealing a bicycle, so it was not a big surprise one sunny afternoon when Bill, who was a few years older than me, got the absurd idea that I was infringing on his territory, an area that included businesses in the vicinity of the Pelican Theater and the Majestic Cafe. To emphasis his point, without warning he swung his armload of papers hard against my head, ringing my ears. Whacked me just like a mobster hit man. Over a one-penny commission, or twenty percent of the cost of a single paper. But, for whatever reason, Bill left the employ of the *Shreveport Journal*/Schultz's Newsstand a few weeks later. No, I didn't ask anyone any questions about his departure and, no, he didn't mysteriously disappear. He was often seen bicycling

I had my regulars that I could count on to buy a paper every day. Four of these worked as mechanics at Emerson Motor Company. When a tornado struck the Haynesville area thirteen miles away, it was big news and the *Journal* covered the event thoroughly. There was no TV then. People who normally did not buy a paper were literally pulling copies from beneath my arm. I tried to hold some back for my regulars, but it was impossible because of the demands from folks who wanted to read everything they could about this storm that had hit so close to home.

By the time I got to Emerson's that day, I had only three copies. Consequently, one of the mechanics, a dark-haired, greasy-faced man in his forties, was left out. I could see in his eyes how unhappy and disappointed he was. He must have felt that I was ungrateful; he was such a steady, loyal customer.

The next day, after things had settled down somewhat and the townspeople had sated their hunger for news, I returned to the car company with an ample supply of *Journals*. As usual, the mechanics bought papers, except for the one who did not get a paper the day before. I asked him if he wanted to buy a paper. He said no. And he didn't buy another paper from me for about five or six weeks. Then I guess he forgave me. He became a regular again, buying a *Journal* each and every day.

One day as I was offering my wares on the local streets, and business was a little slow, I saw our postman, Mr. Theron DeLoach, walking at a breezy pace. "Sir, would you like to buy a paper?" I asked politely.

His answer was two words: "Can't read." And he kept on trucking, not missing a stride. This was around the time that a lot of our mail got sent to Houma.

At the end of each workday I returned to the newsstand and turned in the unsold copies of the *Journal* and my pocketful of pennies, nickels, dimes and quarters, then collected my wages, on average, about twenty-five cents per day. Then I would fight the temptation to spend forty percent of those earnings on a *Roy Rogers* comic book. Most of the time I saved all the money and rationed myself one or two funny books a month.

The Comic Book Capitalist

When I amassed a good supply of those comic books, I sold my entire inventory except for *Roy Rogers*. I simply could not bear to part with those beautiful colored photos of Trigger that graced the front covers. One day I saw an opportunity to really strike it rich. I entered a contest to name Trigger's male offspring. Just like a million other kids I picked the name Trigger Jr., and it won, of course. So a drawing was held to break this huge tie and determine who would get the grand prize. I don't know who the lucky kid was, but I do know that he did not live in Homer. In about a week my consolation prize arrived in the mail. It was an eight by ten color picture of Trigger and his little palomino son, Junior.

One of my best customers when I sold comics for a nickel apiece by a roadside near my house was G.W. Zachary's father, G.W. Senior. He was in local law enforcement, so I figured he needed some good reading material to reduce stress and keep him relaxed. When he stopped his car and looked over my inventory, he didn't just purchase one comic. He bought a whole dollar's worth at one time. A very good customer he was. A repeat customer I might add. If I had had any sense of marketing back then I would have officially named him Customer of the Year. Have it printed up in *The Guardian-Journal*.

The Coke Capitalist

Another sole-proprietorship was my soft-drink business. I got the idea underway by first borrowing money from my dad to purchase a case of 6 ½-ounce Cokes at the Homer Coca-Cola Bottling Plant. When Mr. Joe Robertson sold me the Cokes, he was smiling broadly because the weather was hot. He explained to his up-and-coming fellow businessman that the hotter it was, the more Cokes he sold. "I love hot weather," he said, still smiling. The cost of the Cokes came to about a dollar, less than five cents a bottle, which was the cost in stores around Homer.

After getting the Cokes, my next step was buying a block of ice from James and Bubba Banks' dad at the ice plant. After I did this I then placed a wash tub onto the wagon that I had gotten for Christmas, put the Cokes in the tub, put the ice on the drinks, chipped the ice up with a pick. I was set. That night I set up shop at the foot of Lyon's Hill at the town softball fields. During games I pulled the wagon around and sold the drinks for ten cents a bottle to thirsty people who were happy to pay that price. I quickly emptied the wagon; I could have sold ten times more.

G.W. Zachary's mother, Marie, was a good customer like his dad had been. Between sips of her Coke she asked if I liked Gene Autry or Roy Rogers best. When I said Rogers she made a face and expressed her love for Gene

Autry. It was a tough decision for me because I liked Autry too. In fact, I had seen him in person and Champion in horse at the Municipal Auditorium in Shreveport, where Elvis would later perform in the coming years. I had a good seat and observed that Gene Autry looked just like himself. I wasn't absolutely sure about Champion. He might have been an imposter.

I made $2.40 that night, and that was big money in those days. I paid Dad his dollar, leaving me $1.40 profit, less the cost of the ice. At the end of the day I brought home a little more than a dollar for myself. How I loved capitalism!

The Love Affair With MLB Begins

But I was more than a vendor. I was a trader, too, with a variety of kids, and the guy who seemed to have the greatest number and greatest variety of comic books on the east side of Homer was Kenny Taylor, who by chance also ignited my love for major league baseball. He inadvertently did this by leaving out so that I could see it, a spiral notebook that consisted solely of the varied batting statistics of players like Pee Wee Reese, Carl Furillo, and Joe DiMaggio (who was a great reader of comic books). Kenny had laboriously compiled with his own pencil, page after notebook page, thorough player statistics: times at bat, hits, singles, doubles, triples, home runs, stolen bases, batting averages, walks. I was totally captivated by this beautiful document, and with curiosity, wondered why anyone would spend his time doing such a project. That was the day I fell in love with major league baseball.

At that time I did not root for any particular team. That would come later, innocently in the future, in 1955, when my friend Bobby Flurry casually mentioned that he liked the Cleveland Indians. The year before, in 1954, the Indians had won a record-setting 111 games and the American League pennant, so I saw them as winners. But as soon as I declared my loyalty to this team, they began going rapidly downhill, getting worse with each passing year. Some years they were the laughing stock of the American League. How could such a smart guy like Bobby be so wrong? Today I understand team loyalty much better. Like an invading virus, the Indians swept into my system, became a part of me and, almost against my will, made me love them. I had no choice. A few years later, I tried to branch out and add the Pittsburgh Pirates of the National League to my spirit of allegiance. It didn't take. My short-lived effort was just like trying to fall in love with another person, but coming to the point of knowing that the required, subjective, necessary chemistry will never be. So, the Pirates had to walk the plank. It's been the Indians ever since. True love.

Kenny's comic book collection was diverse, with all the Disney characters like Mickey Mouse, Donald Duck, Uncle Scrooge, as well as Bugs Bunny, Elmer Fudd, Woody Woodpecker, and Andy Panda. He had a lot of D.C. comics as well: Superman, Batman, Wonder Woman, also Captain Marvel; some horror comics and a few crime comics.

Squirrel Brantly, on the other hand, read nothing but war comics like *Frontline Combat, Battlefield Action,* and *Our Army at War.* Squirrel's obsession with war would grow through the years like a mushroom cloud. More about him later.

Taylor's Drive-In

Another job I had was carhopping at Taylor's Drive-In, which was less than a mile from my house, located in a section of town called Little Chicago. (I do not know how it got that name.) Bill Taylor hired me along with Glenn Wilkins and Eugene Watson. Before the novelty of this new adventure had worn off, the three of us got into arguments over which of us would hop the next car. When I got a little aggressive in being the first to a car that pulled up I was accused of just wanting to get the most tips. It wasn't that. I just wanted to work. I wanted to be doing something other than sitting on top of a wooden soft drink case and daydreaming.

In time, just like the business of selling newspapers, I worked alone, the only carhop at Taylor's. People come and people go, I was learning. The biggest problem I faced when it was just me was customers who might drive up to Taylor's in a 1947 Chevrolet, place an order and then climb into the 1948 Ford of some of their friends across the parking lot. On weekends this practice seemed to go on a lot, causing me considerable confusion, and sometimes people became impatient and started blowing their car horns, three or four at the same time. It got to be a little nerve-racking.

Things were slower and quieter weeknights. On one of those nights a man drove up, and I quickly got to the window of his car to take his order.

"Yes, sir?" I said.

He wasn't interested in hamburgers or fries. With glazed eyes and a slurred voice, he said, "Are there any women inside who like to ----?"

I was polite even to drunks. I answered truthfully, "I don't know, sir."

"Well, go in and find out," he said.

All of a sudden I was a thirteen-year-old pimp. I went inside and stayed there until he cranked up his car and drove away.

Willard the Wizard

When I was twelve or thirteen Willard the Wizard came to Homer and set up his two sprawling, gigantic tents just a fraction of a mile down the hill from our house on Keener Street.

I had always been fascinated by magic tricks and stunts. My favorite comic strip character at that time was Mandrake the Magician, whose hypnotic gestures took immediate effect and created hallucinative lions and tigers and anything else Mandrake could dream up and use to subdue his adversaries.

This was before television came to Homer, so, other than the Pelican Theater, there were few local venues for entertainment. Willard brought along in a convoy of seventeen trucks and trailers his staff and his family of wife and daughters. When they climbed onstage to assist Willard with his acts they were appropriately clad in top hats, vests and blousy shirts He was quite good and very professional, with the proud look of a Salvador Dali.

One of his daughters caught my eye at once. Her name was Frances, and in seconds I completely absorbed her. Hair: brownish-blonde of medium length. Eyes: a darker brown than the hair, with a subtle reserve that I could not quite define. Skin: light olive. Nose: diminutive. Age: close to my own, probably a little younger. Personality: unknown. Close proximity and careful observation necessary to determine.

Each morning after breakfast I left home and descended the hill, with the fresh, pleasant blues and yellows of summer morning glories coursing through my senses, and bustled with increasing excitement across Highway 9 onto the sacred Willard soil. The nearness of the encampment allowed me to be on location each day and do odd jobs such as setting up folding chairs for Willard's foreman, Hector, a tanned muscular no-nonsense guy in his twenties. This endeavor provided me with free tickets for each show, where I would simultaneously gaze upon the girl of my dreams and enjoy the entertaining magic of her father.

During slow work periods I stayed around and talked with various crew members about their life of traveling through the states of Louisiana, Texas, Arkansas, and Oklahoma, and, as much as possible, watch Frances who, offstage during the day, wore a freshly ironed sleeveless blouse and Amelia-like tan shorts, quietly wade barefoot in the cool stream of branch water that flowed unhampered under the highway and Keener and continued east. She never seemed conceited about her beauty; she just went quietly about her play with her older sisters.

As the first week of Willard's visit came and went, I burned with a desperate desire to approach her at the creek and ask her to put on her opened-toed sandals and walk to town to the Pelican Theater for a matinee picture show. My fantasy created a marvelous picture of my purchasing our twelve-cent tickets and bags of five-cent popcorn. How that would impress her, I thought, and for that alone, she would want to marry me. Each day I secretly rehearsed the words of this invitation and tried to muster the courage to deliver it. But whenever I got close enough for our shadows to momentarily cross, my tongue turned to solid lead and my quivering lips froze. I was unable to utter a single word. On the threshold of adolescence, I began to realize that there was a vast difference between boys and girls and that beauty can be intimidating for someone facing this realization for the first time.

One night during the middle of the second and final week, and with time running out to shed my cowardice in speaking to Frances, I volunteered from my choice seat in the audience to assist Willard the Wizard with a new act. Getting on stage would place me only mere feet from Frances. Just moments earlier her father had passed a brass ring around her levitating body, and the audience, who paid ten and twenty cents for their tickets, showed their delight with collective gasps and prolonged applause.

When I ascended to the platform, with klieg-like lights shining brightly in my eyes, I seemed to float across the stage on dreamy, surrealistic clouds. I stood next to Willard with revved excitement; I had never been this close to a man wearing a cape. Willard's eyes were intense, his dark hair was parted down the middle of his head, and he was wearing under his black coat a spotless white, collarless shirt with a matching silk bow tie. There was a trace of after-shave with a subtle oaken flavor.

Willard began the skit with a rich timbre in his voice so that even those sitting in wooden, fold-up chairs at the back of the huge tent could easily understand each of his words. "Son, what will you have to drink?"

Then he whispered something to me out of the side of his mouth. Only I could not hear it said. Being hard of hearing put me in panic mode, and the fact that he whispered with his mouth nearly closed like Edgar Bergen prevented me from using my fall-back strategy: reading lips.

When I failed to respond Willard whispered a bit louder. I stared back at Willard like I was totally mute. Willard kept trying, with each try increasing in resonance until those in the first seven rows surely were hearing what I couldn't. On his fourth attempt I finally heard, "Say 'whiskey'."

"Whiskey," I said meekly, feeling like a dodo.

"Louder," Willard whispered back through clenched teeth.

"Louder," I said at a suitable decibel, and as soon as I had spoken the word, realized that I was killing his script. Even without looking at them I could sense massive confusion in the audience.

Willard squinted his eyes in anger, twitching his black mustache. When he did that I said, "Whiskey," in my strongest stentorian voice and sneaked a glance at the audience. They were looking at each other. Some were laughing.

Willard proceeded to pour me a small glass of stale cola and handed it to me. His hand was trembling and I could see the arteries throbbing in his neck. I downed the fake whiskey and when I handed the glass back my hand trembled a little, too. He was a magician; why didn't he just saw me in half and make me disappear?

I don't even remember what the trick was or how "whiskey" fit into it, but when the act was over I left the stage without looking at Frances, but I could feel her eyes following me as I descended the stage step by painful step. I considered just walking out of the tent to my house, but my love for magic was still strong, so I returned to my seat for the rest of the show, thinking there was little doubt that I finally had Frances' attention.

Theaters

In the fifties Homer had three theaters for white folks and one for the blacks. The Caucasian picture shows had names that began with the letter *P*: the old Pelican, managed by Ralph and Mary Martin, just off the Square, with its various nooks and crannies; the newer Paula, on the Square next to the Homer Drug; and the short-lived Pines Drive-in Theater out on the Haynesville Highway.

The movie house for African-Americans was located just off the Minden Road. It was an odd-shaped arched tin building. In earlier years blacks attended the Pelican, buying their tickets at a separate place outside the theater, then going up a separate staircase into the balcony, which was theirs exclusively. But this practice came to an end when blacks were banned from the theater. There were complaints of their spitting off the balcony onto whites seated below. Anyway, that's the story I always heard.

The Paula was owned and operated by Oswald Fomby, who gave the theater the same name as his younger daughter. Fomby used a lot of gimmicks such as drawings for prize giveaways to build attendance. Granddaddy Kilpatrick, who loved westerns, came from Arcadia one Tuesday night to win a pound of bacon during intermission. On Friday nights kids attended in droves to see cliff-hangers like Superman, only we called them "continued pieces." After the first showing, Fomby gave away free bubble gum outside in front of the Paula. He had two laws about these gum gifts: (1) you were allowed to reach into the gum box and withdraw one piece and no more, and (2) once you got your gum you were not allowed to re-enter the theater. Both rules were broken.

When I was a teenager with little cash on hand, John Wayne Odom, Gladney Davidson, and I pooled our change to purchase tickets for the Pines Drive-In. We came up with enough money for two tickets. So it was decided that one of us would hide in the trunk of John Wayne's car; that person turned out to be me. I am not certain about how that happened. Since the car belonged to the Odom family, John Wayne had to be ruled out. He was the designated driver. So Gladney and I considered drawing straws, only there were none around. I think it ended up being that old, "Eeny, Meeny, Miney, Moe," counting rhyme that decided the designated stowaway. I always lost at that game.

John Wayne unlocked the trunk and I climbed in. Then he drove to the ticket booth where I was certain the ticket seller could hear my labored breathing. It was the middle of the summer, after all. It seemed to take forever to complete the simple act of purchasing two tickets. Once that was done, John Wayne slowly drove the car inside and seemed to take his sweet time finding a spot. Meanwhile I was sweating like I was in a sauna and finding it difficult to breathe. At last I heard the motor of the car die. Free at last, I thought. But nothing at all happened. It was as if those two had completely forgotten about me. I kept waiting for one of them to get out of the car and raise that trunk. But I waited on, and at a point I panicked and began to think that this was how it would end for me. The people who went to church every Sunday would shake their heads and say, "Tsk, tsk, it's a shame about Randall Tabor suffocating in the trunk of that car, but he got what he deserved. He was an evil kid. He tried to cheat the Pines Theater."

Finally, just as I imagined that I was taking my final breath, John Wayne raised the trunk. I was grateful that I would live to see the movie, but at the same time I was furious with him, although I knew that he was being careful to keep us from being caught. "What's the matter with you?" I yelled. "I almost suffocated to death."

He looked at me without sympathy and said, "When I go hunting, I put my bird dogs in there, and they don't complain."

Homer Idol

In the early fifties when Hank Williams was the hottest country singer around, Homer had its own Ted Mack Amateur Hour on summer afternoons at the Pelican Theater. It was kind of like today's *American Idol*. People from the audience were encouraged to go up to the stage and showcase their talent. My mother, who always loved music, sometimes attended these events.

Some of the participants seemed quite good to me. However, this was before television, and we were starved for entertainment of any kind. My mother had warned me not to embarrass her by offering my skills on that stage. In earlier months she had chosen others over me in little singing contests held at her kitchen table. I had asked her beforehand not to choose me as the contest winner simply because I was her son, but only because of my God-given talents. At first she said she didn't want to be a contest judge, but we insisted.

We sang through a number of rounds with various songs, and Mom didn't pull any punches in her judging. Like a female Simon Cowell she sent me to the entertainment showers with each and every lyric that I offered. I tried to sing bass, then tenor, then I was a baritone. I considered going alto and soprano, but nothing worked. When I failed to win a single round I realized the sad truth: her son was a musical moron.

Yet, undaunted, I tried to learn to play the flute under the tutelage of Phil Kendall, the Homer High School band director. But when I could not progress past *Mary Had a Little Lamb*, I ended my career as a musician.

Years later, in the fall of 1957, Charlie Roberts came to Homer High School as the new director of music and re-built my self esteem. No, I wasn't one of the guys in the Boys' Quartet, or even the Boys' Ensemble, but I did manage to hide myself in the eighty-member mixed chorus, where my voice managed to get lost and go somewhat unheard. Mixed chorus was one of my senior courses, and apparently singing and hearing good singers every morning Monday through Friday paid off. One day in the spring of 1958 I walked through our house singing somewhat absentmindedly the lyrics from *Around the World in Eighty Days*, one of the songs that Charlie had drilled us on. I didn't know that my mother was listening. "That sounds *good*," she said.

What a comeback, I thought. So today I find myself practicing for *American Idol* in front of my dog Hannah. She's the only who listens for more than five minutes before leaving the room.

High School

Miss Mary Tooke

Because she hated nicknames with a passion, our high school English teacher, Miss Mary Tooke, never called "Butch" Chadwick anything but Phillip. Her classroom was where Butch often came up with zany stuff like trying to convince Miss Tooke of absurd happenings taking place under her nose. One day he interrupted her as she was explaining the subjunctive mood to us. "Miss Tooke, I can't concentrate on what you are saying because someone in the back corner of the room is making noises like a kangaroo." Then he would wave an arm in the direction of the source of the sound, and add, "Over in that general area." That day it was a kangaroo. The next day it might be a giraffe or a monkey. The usual punishment for him was a thrashing with a handful of rolled-up lecture notes. Butch pretended to be in intense pain from the pounding on his head and shoulders and defended himself by covering up with both arms and sobbing, except that he was really laughing and everybody but Miss Tooke knew it.

Later on, before the period was over, Miss Tooke developed deep pangs of remorse for her lack of self-control, and, with teary eyes, announced that it was time to stop what we were doing and pray for Butch. Thus, we were directed to bow our heads and close our eyes and keep them closed until the end of the prayer. Moments later Miss Tooke said, "Amen," and beamed. "I am so proud of this class," she said. "As I was praying, I peeked. Yes, I did. I peeked and saw that every single student in this room had his head bowed and his eyes closed. Even Phillip."

Miss Tooke was the only person I knew who won a major prize in a contest. It was a light blue Studebaker from Reader's Digest. I don't know what she did to win the prize, but her entry must have had something to do with the use of the English language. Or maybe even Spanish, for she taught that language as well. Miss Tooke drove the car so slowly to and from school that it took her through the rest of the school year and into the middle of August to break it in.

Miss Tooke loved to talk about Mexican bullfighting as much as she despised hearing people use nicknames. If we became bored with our English lessons, one of us, (always a model student that she trusted) with a face overflowing with sincerity, politely steered the lesson onto the subject of bullfighting. Mexico and its popular sport was her love, and she, with ease, made her experiences south of the border come alive for us, and in our small-town minds we saw the sleek, proud matador, his muscular opponent, El Toro, and a fanatical, sombrero-wearing crowd cheering, "Ole, Ole ." Each of her stories had their various nuances and vicariously swept us away from our rural Louisiana dwellings and allowed us vivid dreams and hopes of someday experiencing our own realities.

The scene was the same in the 1930s and 1940s when Miss Tooke told the tales of the grand splendor of Mexico to my uncles: Elton, Dude, Hutto, and even to my father, C.L., the oldest of the Tabor brothers. But poor Miss Tooke stayed too long in the classroom and allowed her Phillip, and all the other Phillips with unbridled energy and imagination and mischief, to wear her down and take from her the luster of teaching. Before I graduated she finally called it quits, retired, and drove her little blue Studebaker off into the sunset. I hoped it was bound for Mexico.

Miss Evelyn Holcomb

We didn't dare pull such stunts in the junior and senior English classrooms of Miss Evelyn Holcomb, not even Butch Chadwick. Her reputation preceded her. When I moved from Mrs. Hessie Watson's sophomore English into Miss Holcomb's junior English, I was already intimidated by the tales of her stern, demanding ways.

Miss Holcomb, an attractive woman whose favorite movie was *Love is a Many Splendored Thing*, found love of her own after I graduated, and she became Mrs. Evelyn Hightower. Being a practical person raised by parents who survived the Great Depression, I thought the best thing about this marriage was that she would not have to throw out her stationery and replace those sheets of paper with new letters.

But before then, I went to English III the first day of class in a mild state of fear, knowing how easy it was for me to screw up without even trying. So, I decided to be the model student, if not academic-wise, then in civility.

Miss Holcomb came unsmiling down the aisles between our desks, handing out course outlines and such. When she got to my desk she said something to me (I have since forgotten what it was.). I babbled, "Ma'am, I'm Randall, Ma'am, Tabor, Ma'am."

It was the first time many people had ever heard her laugh. A few smiles here and there, but no laughter. She and I ended up okay for next two years through junior English, senior English, and speech. It was from the latter class in the spring of 1958 that she picked me to go to the North Louisiana District Rally in interpretative reading. No other teacher had ever chosen me for anything since Mrs. Whitlow asked me to lead the first graders into the dreaded netherworld of the grammar school auditorium.

This time I wasn't going to blow it. When I hesitated in giving my answer (yes, a house can run), Glynda Tuggle, who sat in the desk behind mine, nudged my shoulders and said, "Do it." I said yes.

In the preparation time prior to the rally, Miss Holcomb stayed after school working hard day after day with me to refine my presentation, the patriotic *I Am an American.*

From the district rally it was on to state rally in Baton Rouge on the LSU campus where I did the same reading and got a real lesson in how it should be interpreted. The lesson was provided by the entrants from the large schools. Those "readers" were actually Thespians in disguise, especially the kid from Byrd High School, which was considered the top school in Shreveport at that time. I never dreamed that I would be teaching at his school in about four years.

He moved freely at the front of the room, bellowing, moaning, sobbing, gesticulating, dramatizing. His was not a simple reading. It was a John Gielgud performance that would likely move John Gielgud himself to rise from his seat in the audience, applaud, and cry out, "Bravo! Bravo, I say!"

Back in Homer in senior English we were doing our part in the area of the dramatic. It was not of our choosing, but rather that of Miss Holcomb. Before we could pass English IV and, in turn, graduate, she required that we individually one by one stand before the class of 37 onlookers and recite from memory seven difficult lines from Shakespeare.

I had stayed up half the night trying to convert to memory each and every one of those lines that Miss Holcomb deemed important. They are from Scene I of the second act of Macbeth:

"Is this a dagger which I see before me,

The handle toward my hand? Come, let me clutch thee.

I have thee not, and yet I see thee still.

Art thou not, fatal vision, sensible

To feeling as to sight? Or art thou but

A dagger of the mind, a false creation,

Proceeding from the heat-oppressed brain?"

In the spring of 1958 these were just a bunch of words about Macbeth dealing with his overwhelming guilt, and the only thoughts I had about them were learning them by heart, reciting them, and getting back to the safety of my desk. Today as I stand in awe of them and their beauty and power, I can readily appreciate Miss Holcomb's reaction to what happened that day in her classroom.

When it came Sammy Simpson's turn to recite these lines, he strode from his desk to the front of the room just like those who had preceded him. But when he spoke it was:

"Is this a switchblade which I see before me,

The blood underneath my fingernails?..."

That's as far as he got.

"Get out," Evelyn Holcomb said, and Sammy was banished from the room. From the look on her face the rest of us knew that no one else should consider reciting their own unique renditions. Except for the remaining presentations it was very quiet in that room for the next hour. I think some people stopped breathing for awhile.

Miss Holcomb taught us to appreciate great works of beauty and to not belittle them; yet Sammy, in a daring, prankish way, was on his way to giving us a lesson in the beauty and power of satire. I have always wondered what else he had in store for us in his remaining six lines.

Mr. Phil Kendall

In 1953 I was in my first year at Homer High School. At that time Phil Kendall, besides being director of the school band, was the overseer of study hall for the first period. The first period group numbered about six or seven students scattered throughout one of the largest rooms in the building. It took up about half of the second floor. With so few in this room, it felt like being in the Grand Canyon.

I sat fairly close to Mr. Kendall's desk at the front of the room and closer still to the rack of magazines that included *Look*, *Life*, *Colliers*, and *The Saturday Evening Post*, my favorites. I loved magazines and I looked through them in study hall, I think, to put off dealing with schoolwork. I could hardly wait for the newest issue of the *Post* to arrive and wait for Mrs. Sula Barber, the librarian, to put it on the reading stick. Once she did that, my being nearest the magazine rack gave me the best opportunity to be the first to get the publication.

This strategic spot was also next to the long row of tall windows that fronted the building on the south side. Diagonally from my desk across to the back of the other side of the room sat senior Blaine Pittman. With so few people in this room on an early Monday morning, the atmosphere was exceptionally quiet.

I was absorbed in the latest *Post* when Mr. Kendall quietly got off his stool on the west side of the room and sneaked down the boys' side stairs. (Yes, boys and girls were segregated as much as possible, with the boys' lockers and stairs on the west end and the lockers and stairs of the girls on the east end of the building. We also had an unwritten rule about boundaries in regard to how close a girl was allowed to stand to a boy. Strictly enforced. We even ate separately in the cafeteria.)

When Kendall reached the ground floor he headed east toward the girls' side. Once there, he went up the girls' stairs and to the open rear door of the study hall. Then he tiptoed up close to Blaine Pittman's back and yelled, "WHOO-WAH!" My buttocks rose an inch or two from my seat. Blaine's must have soared even higher. I think some people wet their pants.

I wonder to this day what in the world Blaine was doing back there to bring Mr. Kendall to take this action. Back in those days I didn't ask questions.

The following year my study hall was totally different. It was full of students, and Mr. Kendall was still up at the front of the room as monitor.

Eddie Dewees sat next to me on my right in the middle of the room. He and I were individually and separately working the same math problems. He began to have some difficulty and wanted to take a peek at my paper. Kendall, of course, allowed no talking at all and only shallow breathing. In silence I shook my head at Eddie, who became annoyed at my refusal. Suddenly his arm came across my desk and his hand slammed down on my paper with an ear-ringing thud.

Kendall acted at once. "Get out, you two! I'm sending you to the principal!" *Both* of us?

Eddie and I went down to the first floor to Mr. Horace Robinson's office. It was my first visit and I was nervous about it because I hadn't been at Homer High School long enough to get to know our principal. What was he like? What would he do to us? We sat in a couple of wooden chairs for about five or ten minutes before he came in. We told him that Mr. Kendall had kicked us out and told us to see him.

I was pleasantly stunned when Mr. Robinson, without asking *why* we had been sent packing or what we had done, said, "You boys go back up there and tell Mr. Kendall that I said you can use that study hall any time you want to."

Life is indeed full of surprises.

Eddie and I were out of our seats and out the door before Mr. Robinson could regain his sanity. We could not believe our good luck. We did exactly as Mr. Robinson said. When we got back to study hall Kendall was reading a newspaper. We got up close to him and, with a mild effort to conceal our giddy euphoria, repeated, word for word, Mr. Robinson's directive.

Kendall didn't say a word, just returned to his paper, and Eddie and I returned to our study hall desks. What was the deal with Kendall and Robinson? Another question I never asked.

Mr. Kendall directed a fantastic school band. They sounded great, marched in true unison, and looked very classy in their golden military-type uniforms. There must have been a hundred students in it. And Kendall, like a band Nazi, worked them hard, expected perfection and usually got it. I, myself, a non-member, was very proud of it. He must have been, too.

Mr. Kendall was good as a play director, too, and worked as hard directing our senior play as he did drilling the band. The play was called *Stag Line* and I played the role of Mac, who was the best man for an upcoming wedding. Tommy McCalman played the groom-to-be, and Sandra Andrews had the female lead as the bride-to-be. (Sandra is the sister of world-renowned orthopedic surgeon Dr. James Andrews, but we called her little brother Jimmy.)

Kendall scheduled a short preview of *Stag Line* for the entire student body the day before the performance. I was extremely nervous in this brief appearance, but that anxiety paid off. My character, Mac, was an older man who was supposed to be rather sophisticated. Thanks to my nervousness I unknowingly came across well as a sophisticate with believability.

When it was over, Kendall came up to me and looked me straight in the eye and said three words: "You were good."

I was ecstatic, but later I wished he had never done that. His comment went to my head, and I got too relaxed in this role. I suppose that resultant cocky manner came across at our dress rehearsal that night. After the rehearsal Kendall came to me again with that same look and said, "You were out of character." I came down a few notches and regained my former humility. Just in time for the next night.

Today I remember none of my lines, but do remember with clarity one of Tommy McCalman's. In the play his character gets the mistaken idea that something is going on between me and Sandra's character, his intended. The prospective groom (Tommy) goes off by himself to consider this "problem." He is missed by everyone and no one can find him. Panic ensues as the time for the wedding draws near. When he finally returns, he gets a lot of questions like, "Where have you been?" and "What have you been doing?"

He answers this last question by saying, "Riding around, trying to decide what to do." It was a serious reply and deserved respect. But John Randall Tabor, not the character Mac, found this line incredibly amusing and fought hard not to destroy a serious line by cracking up on stage. (Yes, a house can run.) Each time Tommy spoke those words throughout the many rehearsals and even the actual performance before the town of Homer, Randall bit his lip to keep from laughing out loud. Fortunately I didn't laugh. However, that one line, like a song that you can't get out of your head, has stayed with me through the years. And when those eight words come into consciousness, I allow myself that laugh that I suppressed so long ago. As for great, unforgettable lines, "Riding around, trying to decide what to do," rivals, in my opinion, "Here's looking at you, kid."

Mr. H.W. Whatley

Hugh Whatley followed Mr. Robinson as principal and did not spare the rod. I don't remember what landed me in Mr. Whatley's office, but whatever it was, it warranted corporal punishment. I was older now and not as afraid even though I knew it would be painful, and my threshold for pain had not changed.

First, Whatley instructed me to bend over, then grab the sides of my blue jeans and pull downward, making them as tight against my buttocks as possible. Then he opened a desk drawer and took out a board that looked like a sawed-off boat paddle. And it had a series of holes drilled in it. So when he swung it to strike my bottom, a draft of wind flew through those holes and supposedly intensified the pain. I think the concept has something to do with wind drag and probably some retired physics professor somewhere is still collecting royalties with that idea.

After about ten whacks or so, Mr. Whatley ended the punishment and put his weapon away. Then he gave me a look that seemed to say, "Okay, I gave you some good, hard licks and you took them like a man. No hard feelings."

I never had any hard feelings whatsoever. I considered Mr. Whatley to be doing his job as a strong leader, the alpha dog. I respected the fact that in dealing with us teenagers he was never sarcastic, never made us feel small and unworthy. He was a straight shooter.

Football coaches, on the other hand, I think must have gotten together at some bygone coaching clinic, put their heads together, and eventually given birth to the fine art of sarcasm. God knows they were good at it.

Today, for this harmless paddling, Mr. Whatley might be stormed upon by irate parents, sued and sent to prison. I never told my parents about my punishment. I would have been too embarrassed. Besides, if I had told them, I would have gotten a P.S. whacking at home. That's just the way things were done back in the fifties. My, how I miss those days.

The Bill May Era

The person who ignited my interest in playing football was Uncle Dude. His was a simple approach. One day he said, "Why don't you go out for football?" I listened to him. He was one of my heroes. He had been a halfback for the Pelicans in the early forties. In a news story that covered a Homer victory over Haynesville on Thanksgiving day of 1942, *The Guardian-Journal* editorialized somewhat, in praising him: *"In the backfield, Maurice 'Dude' Tabor, the Pels' diminutive halfback, played the best game of his career. His running, passing and defensive work was superb."*

In 1944, when all his friends had been drafted into the military, he went to the local draft board and wanted to know why he had not been called to serve his country. Thus, he ended up in the Army and chose to become a paratrooper for an additional $50 each month. Much of his salary he sent home to help his parents.

He was a member of the 17th "Thunder from Heaven" Division that rescued the famed 101st Division which was surrounded by the Germans. The 17th was the first division to step foot on German soil. On January 24, 1945, when a volunteer was needed to lead his squadron through the forests of Belgium, seven miles from the German border, he stepped to the plate. On the patrol he tripped the wire of a booby trap and when the ensuing explosion brought him down, he knew what had happened. "I'm hit!" he cried to his fellow soldiers. He ended up with a severe abdominal wound that put him in a French hospital. The following March he was summoned to re-join his outfit even though his wound was still leaking.

Perhaps a letter to home can best show who he was. It follows, slightly condensed:

Germany
May 11, 1945

Dear Mom Dad & all

I know you must feel a little better now since these lads have given up. I'm O.K. but I'm still at this Depot trying to get back to my outfit. We didn't think much about the war being over. It was too hard to believe. I wish F.D.R. could have lived until the finish of these dogs.

I was thinking how I would love to catch a plane home so I could be there Mother's Day. I always was good at day dreaming. I can only wish you a happy Mother's Day and I know I have the sweetest <u>Mother</u> in the <u>World.</u> Tell Gracie although she has the sweetest boys in the country it's hard to realize that she is a Mother, too. I hope I'll be home the next time it rolls around to Mother's Day.

Tell Randall and Pluto I'm sorry I haven't sent them any souvenirs, but when moving you don't have much time to think about things like that. I'm sending them some Belgian, French and German money to hold them for awhile.

Tell Son to get that chev. warmed up. I might want to use it one of these days before too long. Tell Elton, Evelyn, Sis, Hut, Chuck, my big Bud, Gracie and Randall that I love them so much that I can't use the right words to tell them how much.

Say, have you picked out the girl for me yet? Ha. Ha. As long as you are my best Girl the rest don't have a chance.

Ask Mary and Ralph Martin I sure would love to slip in the show again. I have been in large theaters in California, Georgia and in England, but I still like that old Pelican Theater best.

I think I'll go see Errol Flynn as a trooper in Burma now. He's not up to his old tricks in this picture.

Lots of Love, "Dude"

Ruston

Uncle Dude got his football wish. When I was fourteen Homer's junior varsity football team hosted the Ruston Bearcats, and Uncle Dude was on the field as an official. Ruston, running from the old, antiquated Notre Dame Box single wing formation that allowed unlimited shifting in the backfield, scored first. They just kept pounding away on our left side with a number of backs leading the way as blockers until they got into the north end zone for a 6-0 first quarter lead.

We tied the score in the same quarter on a pass from Bobby Flurry to me in the southeast corner of the field, close to the school gymnasium. Flurry's pass was right to me, but above my head and I was well-covered, with a lone defender just a foot or two behind me at the goal line. I jumped with arms and hands outstretched and managed to catch the ball, and expected a hit from behind. The defender's hands raked down my back and I stepped backwards into the end zone for the score.

A few minutes later during a timeout Uncle Dude came over to our huddle and, with excitement in his voice, said to my teammates, "Did y'all see that? Did y'all see him make that touchdown? Did y'all see it?"

None of my teammates said a word. And at that moment I wished to be on another planet, preferably Pluto.

What could I say? Uncle Dude was one of my heroes.

My dad was sitting in the stands at the fifty-yard line with Gordon Lee, who ran the Claiborne Drug on the Square. Gordon seemed to center his life around Homer sports and the drug store. When I was in the drug store I always enjoyed listening in the background as Gordon, with the stub of a cigar in the corner of his mouth, told a small gathering some great sports stories while I sipped on a cherry nectar. According to Dad, Gordon had been yelling throughout the game, "Please let Number 33 carry the ball one more time!" That was my number, so I guess Gordon liked how I was playing. He must have obtained some information about my identity. He turned to Dad and said, "Red, is that your boy?"

Neither team could score after the first quarter, so we ended up in a 6-6 tie.

Mom would not go to any of my games when I was that young. She lived in fear of my suffering an injury and could not bear the thought of seeing me sprawled on the gridiron in pain. So she stayed home.

I guess Dad must have been proud of me. (Actually I had a better defensive game that night.) When I got home that Tuesday night, he handed me the keys to his car and a dollar and told me to drive myself somewhere and get something to eat. The dollar was quite sufficient. In the early fifties it could buy a made-from-scratch hamburger, a soft drink, fries, and a milk shake. And you would get change back. The burger cost 20 to 25 cents, the fries 15 to 20 cents, the soft drink 10 cents, and the milkshake 20 cents. That's a max of 75 cents.

I was not yet old enough to have a driver's license, but I had been practicing with my dad's supervision. And I had *never* driven at night under any conditions. When I was in the learning stage I talked Dad into letting me drive from Aunt Gladys' house in Minden to our home in Homer. He agreed to this and the twenty-mile trip went fine until we got to Homer. As I turned from Keener Street into our driveway I misjudged the opening of the garage and ran into the garage door wall. The car was not damaged, and Dad repaired the damage to the wall.

With this blemish on my driving record I was really surprised that he gave me another chance so soon. He believed that nighttime driving was safer. Fewer cars on the road, he reasoned. Plus, you can see other cars because their headlights would be on.

I drove the fraction of a mile down the hill to Bill Taylor's Drive-In. It was closed and even though Dad did not place any restrictions on this deal, I was not going to risk driving across town to The Purple Cow. I turned the car around at Bill Taylor's and drove back home greatly relieved that I got back without any mishaps. Dad seemed a little surprised that I was back so soon. I told him Taylor's was closed and handed him the car keys. He said I could keep the dollar.

The next year I had my license and was getting considerable experience driving the 1954 Buick Century that I had thought we were not going to get. It was our second new car; the 1950 Chevrolet, its predecessor, was our first.

When we first got the Buick, I would get out of bed each morning and go out to the same garage that I had run into last year, open the car door, get in on the driver's side and sit there for a long time just inhaling the new car smell. This was before television.

To buy this car we went to Haynesville with hopes of trading in the Chevrolet. When we first saw it, shiny on the showroom floor, everybody fell in love with it. We were dazzled by the white top that complimented the blue body.

Dad got down to business with the salesman; he went into his gifted horse trading mode. He and the salesman got close but could not strike a deal. Finally, the salesman brought his manager to the negotiating table, but to my disappointment no deal was reached. Dad left his phone number and address and we returned to Homer without a new car. Mom and I criticized Dad for blowing the deal. We thought someone else would step into that showroom and buy it like a loaf of bread. He took our criticism well, and said, "They'll be here at our house tomorrow." Yeah, sure, I thought. The next morning there was a knock at the door at 401 Keener Street and there stood the two salesmen. That day we became the proud owners of a 1954 Buick Century.

Farmerville

We played at Farmerville on a Monday afternoon in the middle of September. I don't remember the start time but I do remember going home for lunch that day and having lots of biscuits, fried ham, and redeye gravy. Probably not the best meal choice a couple of hours before playing football.

We couldn't use the school buses for this forty-mile trip to Union Parish because they were needed to take students home from school. So we had to load up in cars. About half a dozen players and I rode in a van with Mr. Whatley, our principal, behind the wheel. We were the last ones to depart because Mr. Whatley could not leave the school right away. During the trip Whatley took our minds off being late by spinning various tales, something he was very good at.

When we arrived in Farmerville the game was in progress. I dressed as quickly as possible and took a seat on the bench. It was about that time that Errol Beavers, one of our fastest halfbacks, swept right end but stopped during his run to cut back to his left. When he did that he was easily tackled. Coach Garrett half yelled, half muttered with frustration in his voice, "Don't stop!" Immediately the reptilian part of my brain shot me off the bench and next to Garrett. "Put me in, Coach," I said. "I won't stop."

He did, and we ran the same play with me carrying the ball. I didn't slow down for anything, and as I was gaining yard after yard, I felt like I could run forever. This should be good for at least thirty I thought. But during the run I was sailing along out of bounds. The thing Farmerville called a football field would have been better suited for grazing cattle. The out-of bounds lines could hardly be seen, and there were no bleachers to serve as guides. It was not thirty yards but it was a first down.

So we decided to run up the middle. I was at right halfback and John Wayne Odom was the right tackle. When my play number, 44, was called, he said to me, "If I put my hand on the right side of my butt that means I'm going to drive my man to the left, and if I put it on the left side, I will drive him to the right. Run on the side where my hand is." Very simple and intelligent instructions.

Forty-four was easily understood. It meant that the number four back (right half) would run the ball through the number four hole between the tackle and the end. Knowing beforehand which side of the tackle to run on provided a huge advantage. Instead of making that decision after getting the ball. We lined up and John Wayne, crouched in his stance, eased his right hand to his right buttock. Then the ball was snapped and he drove the opposing tackle left and I took the handoff and ran to John Wayne's right side through a hole big enough for a diesel truck. When I got past the line, defensive backs began to converge on me. I didn't slow down. It was much like running through a corn field. You brush against those stalks, but they don't knock you to the ground. That play gained considerable yardage. John Wayne "Rollo" Odom made it happen.

I stayed in the game until the half. At halftime there was an abbreviated game between the younger players. That included me, so when it began I was on that team, too. That was okay with me. I just wanted to play. Then, when the older boys resumed play, I started that game as well.

During the ride home, Mr. Whatley said some nice things about my play, and when we got back to Homer, as I was leaving our dressing room, Mr. Banks, James and Bubba's dad whom I knew as the Ice Man, smiled at me and offered praise as well. He predicted a good future for me.

Nicknames

A significant number of guys who went to Homer High School had nicknames. And most of the names seemed to have been accepted and tolerated in good spirit. Nevertheless, a few were hard to live down. So in presenting the following list of HHS monikers, I exclude surnames. The list includes football coaches. In alphabetical order they are: Bird Dog, Bubba, Buck, Buddy, Bulldog, Butch, Buzz, Cheapie, Duggo, Gubby, Hook-Nose, Jug-Butt, Letterman, Mug, Orange, Pea Head, Peanut, Pluto, Red Rock, Rock, Rollo, Rosey, Satch, Saucer Lips, Shoes, Slickaman, Squealer, Squirrel, Toots, Wombat.

All of these are good Homer names, but none are as accurate as a nickname given to a Haynesville guy by, I suppose, his Haynesville friends. If the Claiborne Parish fair officials judged nicknames as they do canned goods, poultry, and livestock, then Haynesville would easily win the blue ribbon. Not because of originality or cleverness. It would be on accuracy. It must have been really easy to come up with. And even before I heard about the name, some thirteen miles from Haynesville, I thought the guy, except for the ears, looked exactly like a sleepy mule. Thus, the name Mule Callender.

I officially acquired the most viscous of my many nicknames on a fall afternoon in 1953 when I was in the ninth grade in commercial geography class taught by the head football coach, Bill May, whose own appropriate nickname was Bulldog. The class consisted of two girls and about fifteen boys, mostly football players.

Coach May took a brief class break, summoned me to a special chair that he had positioned just inches from his big desk, tapped me atop my head with a three-foot ruler and knighted me: "I hereby dub thee Sir Amber Inn Tabor." Then I was officially assigned that chair for the rest of the school year. If King May needed his knight he only had to reach out.

My knighthood is indebted to Squirrel Brantly, who was the cause of it all. It happened like this: Three days prior to the classroom ceremony the football team, of which I was a small part at that time, stopped at the Amber Inn Restaurant in Bossier City to have a post-game meal after the lowly Warriors of Vivian, about thirty miles north, near the Texas and Arkansas borders, had already feasted on fried Pelican for their repast. Despite their embarrassing loss to a weak team, Homer's "A" squad was served their fried chicken dinners before we "B" teamers got ours. Thus the varsity finished up first, then headed to the ice cream area for milk shakes and sundaes and left for Homer on their bus.

We little guys followed suit, finished eating and stopped for ice cream before boarding our bus. I was last and Squirrel Brantly was just ahead of me. We both ordered shakes. When he got his, my last words were: "Squirrel, tell them I'll be on the bus as soon as I get my milkshake."

Five minutes later I plunked down my twenty cents, grabbed my shake and headed to the bus. Only there was no bus. Of any kind. Anywhere. Stunned, I circled the Amber Inn, hoping the driver had simply moved the bus to another spot. No bus. And no Squirrel. No anything with a connection to Homer, Louisiana, fifty miles away to the far east. And home, fifty miles away for a thirteen-year-old small town kid who had never been anywhere in the 1950s, might as well have been The Far East.

I tried not to cry as I went inside the Amber Inn and called my parents. Eating last has its advantages: my parents had had time to get home from Vivian, and it was wonderful to hear their familiar voices. I was assured that they would be in Bossier City as soon as possible, normally more than an hour's drive before the four-lane highway and Interstate–20 were built. So I sat outside the Amber Inn and waited. During the wait a couple about my parents' age drove up. They must have wondered why a kid my age was sitting by himself outside the Amber Inn after eleven o'clock. They struck up a conversation and I told them what happened. The lady reminded me of my mother's cousin Ruth, who ran a beauty shop in Monroe. She had outstanding comforting skills, and I think she wanted to take me home with her. She and her husband stayed with me until my Dad drove up forty minutes later. On the drive home my mother said, "She looks just like Cousin Ruth."

The next day I phoned Squirrel, who lived a fraction of a mile down the hill from our house, exactly where Willard the Wizard put on his magic show years back. Squirrel put me on hold for what seemed a very long time. I was about to hang up when I saw Squirrel's face peering through our screen door, his eyes watching me hold the phone to my sore ear.

He thought his explanation was simple and understandable. And that was that when he boarded the bus the previous night, hands and mouths of all kinds and shapes flew at him in a concerted effort to get some of that milkshake. Squirrel lost focus. It was either saving that shake or me, the future knight of Homer High School, Sir Amber Inn Tabor.

After Squirrel's milkshake dilemma was resolved the driver was already on his way to Homer. "We tried to tell the driver, 'We've left Tabor at the Amber Inn,'" Squirrel explained, "but I guess he didn't believe us. He kept going."

So the following Monday Bulldog May created Amber Inn Tabor and that name took hold and spun off into various mutations such as Sir Amber, John Amber and The Amber Inn Kid. They say that time heals all, but two years later sportswriter Gladney Davidson would not allow forgetting as he wrote in the *Prattling Pel* school newspaper, "Amber Inn Tabor scored twice on pass plays."

Even in more recent years the following kind of dialogue would be heard: "Do you know Randall Tabor?"

"Yeah, I sure do. He's the guy who ambered in and staggered out, back in fifty-three." I suppose *ambered* was some kind of clever play on words. Anyway, I heard *ambered* a lot.

Squirrel Brantly, tall and lanky, liked, to a degree, playing end on the football team, but he absolutely loved playing war. Most kids in their spare time would go outside and practice shooting baskets. Squirrel spent his time digging foxholes in his backyard. Obsessed with military battles, Squirrel had his room filled with war comics. One day, his posture militant, he coaxed me into playing a game in which it was my task to "rescue" him from somewhere deep behind "enemy lines" in the woods behind his house. After about twenty minutes of searching I finally found him lying face down on the ground, uncomfortably still, stretched out like an old dog. As soon as I touched him, in total seriousness he said, "You're dead."

"What do you mean I'm dead?"

"My body was mined." Then he puffed his mouth and created a booming explosion. I gave him a D-plus for sound effects and an A-minus for imagination.

Last I heard, Squirrel had grown to almost seven feet and was a cop in Monroe. Whether he ever became a Marine, which was his life dream, I don't know. Hope so because Squirrel loved war almost as much as General Patton. Maybe more.

Two other nicknames were spawned in Coach May's class. I'm not sure which came first. Actually they were sorta born like twins. Minutes before Coach May arrived at the classroom, an altercation broke out between Tommy Goodwin and Phillip Chadwick, who already had the nickname Butch. Tommy gave him a new one: Hook-Nose. Phillip retorted with "Saucer Lips" for Tommy. They almost came to blows there and then, but Coach May's arrival caused a postponement. The future pugilists agreed to have it out by meeting at the theater later that night, only no one said which theater. Nevertheless, I was not about to miss this showdown. I made arrangements to go to the Pelican Theater with Tommy and his little brother Jerry that night. When Butch did not find Tommy at the Paula Theater on the north side of the Square, he headed to the Pelican Theater, south of City Hall Auditorium. Tommy, Jerry and I were somewhat absorbed in the movie, thinking Butch was not going to show up, when there he was, saying to Tommy, "You ready?"

Outside on the sidewalk it was like boxing promoters trying to decide on the site for the heavyweight championship. I took one look at that hard concrete under our feet and quickly suggested that the bout be held in the Coca Cola park where knockdowns might be cushioned by soft springtime grass. The combatants agreed to that site and the four of us, like lifelong friends, strolled to our destination, all the while chatting amiably about sports and girlfriends and teachers. After we had passed Schultz's Newsstand and turned east past DeLoach's Esso gas station we were halfway there.

At the park "Saucer Lips" and "Hook–Nose" removed their shirts to reveal their bare torsos, squared off and without delay began hitting each other. "Splat, splat, splat," were the sounds that told me that this was no picture show at the Pelican. In only seconds it was clear who was going to win this fight. Better not ever call Tommy Goodwin "Saucer Lips." He looked like a polished, professional prize fighter. Butch continued to take the blows until Tommy, with a trace of sympathy in his voice, said, "You had enough?" Butch nodded and mumbled something that I could not hear. Whatever it was it meant yes.

The fighters put on their shirts and the four of us strolled out of the park in the same amiable manner, and Tommy and Butch seemed to be good friends. Then the winner focused on Jerry and me. Sternly giving us a severe stare, he said, "Listen, you little bastards, I don't want a word of this at school tomorrow. Keep this under your hats. Understand?" Of course we understood, even at our young age, the merits and valor of honor and sportsmanship. Besides, we had just seen this guy deal out some severe punishment. This night he was alpha dog. Jerry and I solemnly promised to keep quiet.

We kept our promise. However, the secret of Butch's beating got out. The next morning Dad dropped me off at school, and as I soon as I stepped from the family Buick, I noticed the crowd around Tommy. As I got closer I heard the familiar sounds of the broadcast of a boxing match. It was Tommy giving a blow-by-blow account of last night's main event. Guess he wanted to make sure that it was told right. And there was Butch standing a respectable distance away, alone, looking down, talking to no one.

Encore! Encore!

Jerry and I moved on and flirted with a vaudeville-like career with a short-lived hambone duet show. Although I had had no professional training in this area somehow I was coaxed into performing with Jerry an Amos and Andy type act at the high school talent show. Rumor has it that Bo Diddley invented the art of beating the hambone, a rhythmic knee and chest slapping of the outer thigh (the hambone), then the top part of the inner thigh, then down again to make a three-beat rhythm. Jerry and I introduced the show with some zany semi-ad lib dialogue, then moved to the music by adding open-mouth slapping and singing "Hambone, hambone, where yo been? 'Round the corner and back again." The audience, the student body and faculty, roared with laughter and really got into the groove.

A few weeks later we were asked to do an encore at a town talent show in the city hall auditorium. I had managed to do the high school performance the one time and retain a bare shred of my dignity. I was not going to risk surrendering that shred by pressing my luck. I turned down the request despite a lengthy plea from Jerry to change my mind. Somebody stepped in for me; I don't who, and I didn't much care. Anyway some folks said later that Hambone II was not as good as the original. The sequel never is. I never beat the hambone again in public.

Each year we held this school talent variety show, and when Audis Gill became our head football coach he volunteered his talents as a singer. I don't recall what song he selected for his solo, but he didn't sound too bad. My mom probably would have rated him fairly high.

Commercial Geography

My special assigned seat in commercial geography put me in a position to witness the cheating of Rock Tuggle on the mid-term exam. To my astonishment Rock had placed his open textbook across his knees and happily copied the answers. Could he have believed the exam was an open-book test? If that were so, then why were all the other students leaving their books closed, including me? Either Coach May's eyesight had suddenly begun to fail, or the fact that Rock was a starting tackle on the football team created a bit of selective vision for Coach May.

The following spring when Homer weather vacillated between mornings and evenings that were cool, and afternoons that were warm and balmy, Margie Callender, one of two girls in commercial geography, spoke in class for the first time. When the peaceful shafts of classroom light disappeared behind scribbles of clouds, Margie, sitting alone in the back of the room, became chilled. The heavy, raised windows briefly gave the rest of us, clothed only in tee shirts, an invigorating, refreshing breeze. But to Margie, wrapped in a heavy gray shawl, the air was a cold and vicious Siberian snowstorm, a rushing gale that enveloped her and slashed at the pores of her numbing skin. She tried to discipline her voice but the words came out as a sudden, high-sonic, shrieking croak: "Coach, it's cold in here!"

May was quick with his gruff order. "You boys put those windows down." We did so, but it was Peanut Covington who returned to his seat and allowed his tongue to droop from his mouth and his eyes to glaze over with an exaggerated look of heat exhaustion. All of us wanted to complain, but one did not question the commands of Coach May.

Despite our thoughtfulness, Margie left us. Before the school year had ended she married an obscure older man none of us knew anything about. The consensus was that the mystery groom was the same fellow that we had occasionally seen necking with Margie in the dark balcony of the Pelican Theater, offering his skinny neck for the comfort of Margie's tilted head, all the while the lovers' fingers entwined.

May's Coaching Style

Essentially a football player could screw up in that class, but on the gridiron, even the practice field, there was little tolerance for error. In fact, May had told me that. A former quarterback/fullback/placekicker for LSU from 1934–36, the El Dorado, Arkansas native sometimes dropped his gruff manner and showed a silly sense of humor at practice. One of his favorite jokes was to call a pre-practice meeting by gathering his players close around him as he squatted near the ground. When the group was sufficiently close-knit May began a noisy series of farts and dared anyone to leave the "meeting."

Under Coach May we were on the honor system, but also watched by the team captain, to run, prior to the start of practice, four laps around the one-fifth mile, broken-down track that circled our practice field. The oval was about two-thirds ancient, worn-down cinder gravel and one-third grass and dirt, with the back of the visitors' football bleachers jutting away from the actual game field out over most of that one-third space. In addition, in the same area there was something of a small trough that ran from the bleachers into the practice field. You had to remember to watch for that each time you circled the field. Naturally we were not able to host any track meets.

Coach May's assistant was Bill Garrett, who when he was first offered the job, exclaimed, "You mean coaching the coloreds?" He was totally blown away with disbelief when was told that he would be in charge of guiding the football fortunes of young Caucasians.

At each practice, May and Garrett would observe our lengthy regimen of calisthenics, walking between us to make sure that everybody was keeping up and doing the correct number of reps. We would begin with the easy ones like side-straddle hops and progress to deep knee bends and never-ending, painful sit-ups, all the while wearing helmets, shoulder pads, hip pads, thigh pads, and knee pads. These daily exercises were especially brutal in the August heat of two-a-days when most of us came back from summer vacation totally out of shape. From time to time I still hear those groans, gasps, grunts, sobs, and cries from abdominal pain and shortness of breath.

One day during this ritual of conditioning in the summer heat, a baritone voice emerged from a nebulous spot in our group as we lay on the ground repeatedly crunching our midsections up and down, up and down, again and again and again: *"It only hurts for a little while. That's what they tell me. That's what they say..."* Then in mid-crunch another voice joined the original, a moment later still another, then one, a bit off-key, added itself to the first three. Like a wave, the singing moved from player to player until the entire squad was crunching and singing and harmonizing all the world like the Norman Tabernacle Choir. I'm not sure, but I do not believe coaches May and Garrett ever blended in. None of us became professional singers, but every single one of us was in shape by early September.

In the 1950s the Louisiana High School Athletic Association allowed athletes to have themselves held back a grade and still be eligible to play their senior year even if they were already eighteen. Or some simply failed on purpose. The caveat was that you could not use either of those methods once you got to the ninth grade. Before then, no problem.

One of the ways that you could screw up with May was by failing that freshman year. "You little piss ant," he would say to the offender, "why didn't you fail the EIGHTH grade so that I could have you for another year of football?!"

May frequently embarrassed his players. Despite the fact that our practice uniforms were laundered by the managers no more than weekly, even during summer two-a-days, there was a limit to May's olfactory tolerance, and he seemed to blame the athletes for this. One hot, humid August afternoon before practice he ordered the entire team to move (a la a funeral procession) single-file by Peahead Prator's* locker, pause, put our heads inside and inhale deeply. May declared it to be the worst-smelling locker in the dressing room. A glum, embarrassed Prator said, "I know it stinks, Coach."

Then there was poor Richard McComic, at the top of the nice guy list and at the top of the depth chart at fullback. What follows is the story of poor Richard.

Coach May didn't believe in athletes having girlfriends. He felt that we should think only about football and not about some little girl who only gave us "pee hards." And during football season he practically forbade such a liaison and grimaced with disapproval each time a lass walked her boyfriend–football player off the field after a game. There was no tolerance at all if the girl was from a rival school such as Haynesville, Minden or Ruston. This was being disloyal to your school.

The scene was Pelican Stadium. The opponent: the Minden Crimson Tide, twenty miles toward Shreveport. Before the kickoff Richard McComic's Minden girlfriend not only approached him on the field but brought along her Brownie Target Six-20 and got Richard to pose in his game uniform for snapshots. This he seemed to willingly do in a good-natured gesture. Click! Click! Click! Click! went the little camera. Unfortunately the photo shoot did not go unnoticed by May. Richard lost his starting job at fullback that night and didn't get off the bench.

Also, Bill May was prejudiced. It was my feeling that May distrusted newcomers who transferred to Homer. I believe he doubted their loyalty to the team. When the Nicholson brothers, Richard and Charles, moved from Logansport to Homer and tried out for football it was obvious that they were treated differently by May. He was more demanding with them and less tolerate. Finally, during practice one day, Richard tore his helmet off and slammed it to the ground. "You can have this uniform," he said to May and walked off the field.

I'm not sure what Pete Moore did at still another practice to get May riled. Maybe Pete's biorhythms were out of whack that day. Maybe he was shying away a bit from the hitting and getting hit during a scrimmage. It's speculation. Anyway, after the dust had settled after a play, May's voice boomed, "Pete, are you scared?"

Pete's answer was normal, but the velocity of his reply seemed curious. It was if he had long anticipated May's question and had his answer on tap. It sounded something like this: "Pete, are you scareNo, sir!"

May tried to get players to rat on each other. One day I heard him ask guard Johnny Ebarb, "Johnny, does Louis (Bufkin) smoke?" I think May already knew that Johnny smoked. He just wasn't sure about Louis, our team captain. Johnny got into more than his share of trouble, but he always seemed truthful in acknowledging his guilt. He acknowledged Louis' as well. He told May that yes, Louis did smoke.

Johnny was the only high school athlete I know to play half a football game drunk. One look into Johnny's watery red eyes and a smell of his breath when he arrived at the dressing room before a game against Minden told us all we needed to know. But his loose, fierce, first–half defensive performance of reckless abandon that night made the all–district team for him. Time and time again he tackled Minden's mammoth all-state fullback Kenneth Beck for little or no gain. Johnny just could not be blocked. Everywhere the lumbering Beck ran, Johnny was there to stop him. A huge underdog, Homer trailed just 12-6 at the half. At halftime Johnny sobered up, and Minden made some sobering adjustments. Final score: 38-6. Louis joined Johnny on the all-district team. Two smokers.

May liked the little guys, the small fries. This was good for me because I was a member of that fraternity. I think his philosophy was that a little guy naturally compensated for his lack of size by having a big, courageous heart. Which, in May's mind, won ball games in the fourth quarter.

One of May's favorites was miniscule running back "Duggo" Fincher, who proved May's theory. Fincher could be knocked down and knocked out but he always regained consciousness and came back and gave his best with courage.

G.W. Zachary

I think May would have liked G.W. Zachary, who was in the ninth grade May's final year as football coach. In a way they were a lot alike. A stocky fullback, with May's same type of toughness, George Washington Zachary Jr. preferred to run over people rather than around them. He seemed to relish contact. Maybe that's why as a player later at Northwestern State College he got some teeth knocked out tackling an Arkansas Razorback.

One of my best Gubby Zachary memories is from 1959. He and I were watching a Homer football game, he home from Northwestern and me from Louisiana Tech. We were not seated together, but I was close enough to hear him, as we sat on the visitor's side of Pelican Stadium, where the Pelicans were playing Minden. Suddenly on the field there was some type of fracas following a tackle near the sidelines on the Homer side near the fifty-yard line. Red flags flew. And Minden was penalized for kicking a Homer player. G.W. happened to be in the midst of three or four boys who were perhaps ten or eleven years old. I heard G.W. speak. It was like a growl. "If that boy kicked me like that, I would whip the whole Minden bench."

The kids were awestruck. One asked G.W., "The whole bench, G.W.? The whole bench?"

Without taking his eyes from the field and his chest swollen with pride, Zachary assured the kids that they had not misheard: "The whole damn bench."

Another G.W. Zachary quote was sent to newspapers by the Associated Press. It follows: "Louisiana's Governor James H. Davis, author of 'You Are My Sunshine,' has been 'defied' by a 2 1/2-year-old Sunday school student. Taught in class that 'God made it rain,' and in review, asked 'Who made the sun shine?' young G.W. Zachary, Jr., answered: 'Jimmie Davis!'"

In October of 1955, Minden had their own G.W., a junior varsity player who found his way into our dressing room twenty minutes before the kickoff. We had beaten him and his teammates earlier that season in Minden, 20-0. Now they were on our turf for a re-match.

His presence certainly got our attention as we were dressing for the game. He stated the reason for the unexpected visit. In the earlier game someone on our team, he said, had hit him with a cheap shot and he was in our dressing quarters to settle the score.

I felt his sudden appearance must have been unprecedented at any level of athletic competition. Anyway, he went about our dressing room as if he had built it himself. Finally satisfied that his adversary was not on the premises he departed with his two lieutenants following him out the door. Where were our coaches? More importantly, where was our G.W. when we needed him? Turned out that this nefarious visit didn't intimidate us. We beat them again, 18-6.

Billy Charles Windsor

During a lively scrimmage one afternoon I ran the ball unfortunately into the zone of Billy Charles Windsor, Homer's version of Arnold Schwarzenegger. Windsor had secondary muscles perched atop his primary muscles. Windsor hit me so hard I immediately lost my breath. As I lay in the grass struggling to breathe there was Coach May hovering over me. Calmly he grabbed my belt and lifted my torso up, let me down, lifted up and let down. Immediately and, I thought, miraculously, my breathing returned to normal. I was okay; I bounced up, ready to resume the scrimmage. May's eyes twinkled. "Hell, you can't hurt a Tabor."

Billy Charles Windsor lived in a small row house with his mother and younger sister, LaVerne, who was a freshman when he was a senior. On fall Friday nights Mrs. Windsor often hitched a ride with my parents and traveled in their 1954 Buick to see her son play football at places like Shreveport, Haynesville, Olla, Mansfield, Monroe, Minden, and Springhill. Billy was always very polite to my parents and showed them great respect.

This respect he held for everyone, even little eighth-grade boys, who basically regarded him as a physical monument. He never took advantage of kids like these as some of the seniors did, like stuffing their small, round-shouldered bodies into their own narrow lockers, closing the metal doors on them, and giggling with delight. Windsor would have none of that.

Then came the era of the Billy Windsor position-switch on the football field. One day he decided that he no longer should be the starting right guard, but, instead, with his combination of speed and strength, the starting fullback. This was a good idea on paper, but his eyes, encased in thick spectacles surrounded by rubber molding so that he had the appearance of a Japanese kamikaze pilot, presented a small problem. Sometimes, when the football was handed off to Windsor he failed to determine who was who in his pathway, and as a result, ran over his own blockers. Kinda like friendly fire on the battlefield. But it could have been worse. Windsor could have lost his bearings and run the wrong way, I suppose, but the goal lines that he crossed were always the correct ones.

Windsor loved women and I believe they loved him. He had a charming, attentive way with them. In his presence they knew for certain that they were women, a special species in his eyes. He was aggressive with them while simultaneously putting them on a pedestal. His style couldn't be copied. It was exclusively his without his filing for the copyright. His, lock, stock and barrel.

The fact that he had no means to transport them around Homer didn't faze him. Either they used her car or he managed to get a teammate friend to chauffeur them for hours around nighttime Homer while he and Miss X smooched in the back seat.

Teammate Peanut Covington, who didn't have a car either, likened Windsor to the actor Stephen Boyd and his role in the 1950s movie, *The Best of Everything.*

May's Final Season

In 1954 May served his final year as Homer's head football coach. He lost his job after sweating out a one-win season (a 27-12 upset of Mansfield at Pelican Stadium). Things had been going so badly that year that May announced in the Homer *Guardian-Journal* newspaper his intention to start the "B" team the next day against defending state champions Springhill because he felt that the second-team Pels had outperformed the varsity in practice.

My Uncle Dude Tabor had read the article and said to me, "May is not really going to start the second team against Springhill is he?" I believed that he would.

May was true to his published promise. His second team lined up against the powerful Lumberjacks, who had recently graduated John David Crow, a Heisman Trophy winner at Texas A&M. After two or three quick Springhill touchdowns, May put the first team into the game and they played competitively. But it was too late. The game was over in the first quarter.

A starting guard for Homer that night was fourteen-year-old fuzzy-cheeked John David Brantly. After the game, John David said that when he looked up from his stance on the field, he was startled to see that his opponent had a beard (five o'clock shadow). "He needed to SHAVE!"

May stayed on the next year as basketball coach and his stubbornness stayed too. When he thought he was getting a raw deal from the game officials at a tournament in Junction City, he abruptly escorted his players off the basketball court in the middle of the game and headed to Homer.

Where the gods of football turned their backs on Bill May, the gods of basketball smiled upon him. They gave him the gift of talented Ronnie Prince. Early on it was obvious that Ronnie had the ability to start on the varsity, but he was an outsider who had recently moved to Homer, not home–grown the way May liked his players. Therefore, Ronnie was assigned to the junior varsity where he easily led that team in scoring. In the varsity games that followed, May slowly began to bring Prince off the bench more and more. Even in a substitute role Prince often led the varsity in points scored. He had a great attitude, kept his mouth shut, didn't complain, and paid his dues. May liked that. Soon Ronnie was starting for the varsity and helping his team win games.

Bulldog May was the consummate tough guy who feared nothing, but it wasn't always that way. He often told the story of his childhood experience of seeing a black person for the first time. "I had never seen a Negro," he said. "The experience totally frightened me. I ran away from him. I ran home."

Eddie Simpson

Before Eddie Simpson and I became friends I simply observed him unselfishly passing the basketball to his grateful teammates and making acrobatic shots in the old box-like gymnasium that sat on the second floor atop the Homer High School cafeteria. Visiting players unaccustomed to the place must have had attacks of claustrophobia when they were introduced to the wooden backboards and the in-close, rectangular wall of brick just mere feet from the out-of-bounds stripe. It was somewhat daunting, except for those like Eddie, a slim, dark blond forward whose motif was twisting, entertaining moves to the home-team basket. Eddie, having grown up on basketball in this strange, unorthodox construction, felt very much at home here.

This site is where my girlfriend Angela* and I sat together on the south side wooden bleachers, hearing the raucous cheers of the opposing fans, but rarely seeing these people because of another unique feature of the ancient edifice: no seats at all across the gym's floor on the north side, just a brick wall that ran from the waxed floor to the top of the arena. The wall featured two things: decrepit steam heaters and a scoreboard whose main features were a rotating black wand that gave us a good idea of minutes remaining to be played and, at best, a vague idea of the seconds. Sometimes the wand moved a couple of seconds past the numeral twelve before the horn blared, officially ending the quarter.

It was on top of one of these highly placed heaters that someone, during a physical education class, tossed the tennis shoes of John David Mitchell. There the shoes sat baking with heat until, with pole and ladder, they were rescued. The event quickly led to Butch Chadwick giving John David the moniker "Shoes" Mitchell. It was a name that captured the fancy of the student body and stuck to John David like glue.

Angela and I sat side by side about halfway up the dilapidated wooden sections that pretended to be seats, but, in fact, felt like hard pine benches, when suddenly someone tapped me on the shoulder from behind. It was Joe Randall "Toots" Atkins. He seemed to be blushing about something but it was hard to know for sure that it was a legitimate blush because his rosy-cheeked face was something of a regular fixture that complimented his rotund figure, sleepy blue eyes, and blond-red hair. He and I were friends but not that close. Right away he came to the point of the shoulder tapping. "I'll give you a quarter if you put your arm around her," he whispered with a goofy, thin smile.

Angela, who consistently held herself like a queen, was from a prominent, well-to-do local family and was brought up with the strict Southern values specifically custom-made for the teenage girls of Homer, Louisiana. Values that frowned on any public display of affection, no matter how innocuous.

Twenty-five cents in those days was significant for a non-income producing teenager. It could buy the January issue of BOY comics and fifteen packages of peanut butter and molasses Kits. It wasn't a bet so I had nothing to lose, but I had no idea how Angela would react to my touching her in public like that. I had never committed such a dastardly act. I gave her a sidelong, furtive glance to check out her mood. She seemed focused on the game, so I made my move, arching my right arm over her back and slowly dropping it to her virginal shoulder. Angela stayed fixed on the game and did not react in any dissuading manner. In fact, a subtle, illusive smile graced her lips. I believe she might have been a little pleased.

I looked back for my quarter and, without delay, it passed from Toots' puffy hand into my own. Even if he had reneged on the deal it would have been okay because I had thoroughly enjoyed the danger-excitement and felt quite pleased with my accomplishment, a major advance in my relationship with Angela.

Eddie Simpson, a couple of grades ahead of me, was a cheerleader as well as a roundballer, the former an elected position. In the spring when he was a junior Eddie decided to try out for football for his final year of school. We seasoned players didn't expect much from him. After all, he was a cheerleader. Plus, we all knew how he had fallen for that greenhorn prank. Here's how we worked it: on day one of Eddie's baptism into spring practice football, a designated veteran of respect innocently eased next to our rookie in the dressing room right after Eddie had been issued shoes, socks, jersey, pants, helmet, shoulder pads, hip pads, thigh pads and knee pads. "Hey, Eddie, where's your titty protector?"

"Huh?" Eddie replied.

"Your titty protector. I don't see it there."

"I need a titty protector?"

"Of course. We all wear titty protectors. You need to go back to the manager and tell him that you didn't get your titty protector."

At once Eddie returned to the manager who had issued his equipment. "I didn't get my titty protector."

The manager's smirk showed that he had been down a similar road numerous times. In matter-of-fact fashion, he said, "We don't have titty protectors. And, believe it or not, we don't even stock bras and girdles."

At this point there was no holding back the laughter from the entire team from seniors to eighth graders. But Eddie was a great sport about the prank and eventually won total respect from all of us on the practice field. When we scrimmaged, Eddie was tried at linebacker and his consistent, hard, crisp tackling got everybody's attention. He was really good and everybody knew it. He performed like he had had years of experience.

As the springtime practice days approached an end, cheerleader elections loomed in the immediate future. Everybody assumed Eddie would not be a candidate, but, alas, they assumed in error. Our projected linebacker announced that if the student body re-elected him, then he would be their cheerleader. We begged him to reconsider. When that move failed, we went to the girls and the guys who were not football players. "Please don't vote for Eddie. We need him on the football field. He can really help us." They rejected our pleas, and despite the energetic, vigorous cheers of our mythical strong side linebacker the following fall, the football team suffered through another dismal, losing season. And I exclaimed in my best Marlon Brando to no one in particular, "Ed coulda been a contenda!" Nobody laughed.

A few years later Eddie and I, along with a couple of other Homerites, commuted to Louisiana Tech, in Ruston, for a semester. One afternoon as our group waited by the car for the driver to get out of class so that we could return to Homer, Eddie demonstrated his skill at understanding human behavior. About forty yards from us we observed a shapely, lavishly attractive coed, books in arms, walking south past Keeney Hall. Wearing a tight, high-waist, straight-fit skirt she moved lightly but with enough hip sway to pull the skirt in alternate directions. A young man in jeans and loafers was alongside her pathway, a leg propped indifferently against a fire plug.

Except for Eddie, none of us saw anything noteworthy. Then Eddie advised us: "See that guy. When that girl passes him, he's going to turn around and take a good look at her." We waited. The girl passed. The guy pivoted. Took a good look. Eddie continued to have our respect.

A Shave and A Haircut

Two things were forced on football players who had not already acted on their own volition: the first shave and the first flattop. They were prescribed by the senior members of the team, who made all the decisions that affected team uniformity. Dressing alike in gold or white jerseys and white pants with purple and gold trim and gold helmets was not sufficient. Everybody on the team had to have a flattop. The gods of the gridiron wished it so.

Wisely, I shaved at home before the football mob could get their hands on me. I had seen beforehand the faces of those whose peach fuzz had crossed out of the no-shave zone and the aftermath hatchet jobs of the mob, whose members simply held transgressors down, lathered them up , and scraped their faces.

While I moved quickly with the shave, I was a bit tardy with the flattop and began to get overt threats like, "Tabor, if you don't have a flattop by Thursday, we are giving you one." They had the clippers right there in the dressing room to back up their threats.

I determined that the guy to transform my head would be Homer's maestro of the comb and clippers: Rex Young. So, in the fall of 1955 I walked into the barbershop across the street from City Hall and uttered the words, "I'm changing to a flattop." Climbing into Rex's chair and allowing him to alter my appearance was one of those experiences that you are initially unsure about, but after it's done, you're glad you did it. Like your first time to ride the Matterhorn at the state fair.

The flattop provided instant gratification in the form of complete and total acceptance from the mob. I felt like I belonged as an integral part of an important group. My black hair spiked straight up like the markings of a Brookshire's bar code, I was now one of them, heart and soul. And being one of them gave me the power and privilege of joining ranks with those who issued threats to the few remaining unitiated.

Everyone loved the masterpiece that Rex did with my lopsided head, except for Grandma Kilpatrick, who deemed Rex's work of art as the ugliest haircut she had ever seen. Despite Grandma's lack of appreciation for "shear" genius I stayed with the flattop for many years into the sixties.

Coach George Hardy Robinson

After May and Garrett stepped down as football coaches Bobby Flurry and I were coached by the new JV coach, George Hardy Robinson, who had been the mayor of Homer. An olive-skinned robust man with energy and a penchant for designing some aggressive football plays. None were plays that the varsity had in their playbook.

In a game in Minden, Jimmy Andrews (now renowned orthopedic surgeon Dr. James Andrews) came off the bench as a backup quarterback to execute one of Robinson's creations. From the right halfback position I zigzagged right, then left a bit over the middle, then back out to the right flat and found myself wide open. Jimmy's pass was the best aerial ever thrown to me. It was perfect, with good loft. It was the easiest offensive touchdown I ever scored. And we won, 20-0.

Just before a game at Springhill Coach Robinson said one thing to me: "Randall, I want to see you bleed tonight." Too bad he wasn't around a year or two ago for that Ruston game in which I fielded a punt and quickly plotted my return to the south end of the field. A big Bearcat was bearing down on me, and I wondered, for a big guy, how did he get downfield so fast? I faked a move left, then right, then ran left past him, hearing him as he missed me, mutter, "Aw, shit!" I raced down the sidelines by our bench for good yardage before getting smacked hard by two or three guys in maroon and gray, Ruston's colors back then. When I got up, blood was pouring from my nose.

Donald Wilkins, the manager, took me into the dressing room and sat me on the training table. As he was working on me to get the bleeding to stop, he said, "Randall, you're shaking." He was right, and even though I seemed to have no control over it, it shamed me. Why was I shaking? Was it nerves? Exhaustion? Excitement? I tried to forget about it and returned to what was going on outside. This shaking thing never happened again.

I tried to bleed for Coach Robinson in that Springhill game, but the only thing I could muster was an old-fashioned bell-ringing. Fairly early in the game I caught a short pass from Bobby Flurry and right away I was hit hard. I never saw the tackler; maybe it was tacklers. Whoever, he/they rang my bell, and I lay on the turf and was very slow in getting up.

Coach Robinson came out and wanted to remove me from the game. Right away, his remark about bleeding came to mind, so I refused to come out. I shook the cobwebs from my head and talked him into letting me stay in.

To make matters worse, those Springhill guys were outscoring us. Seemed like for every one of our touchdowns, they made two. But with us trailing just 24-20, Kenneth Hood, one of our guards, almost enabled us to catch up. On an off-tackle play I carried the ball downfield on the far side of the field from our bench behind what I thought was a terrific block by Kenneth. It was a long run from scrimmage that got us close to their goal. When it was called a clip, my frustration increased. We could not catch a single break.

Then in the fourth quarter, a Springhill running back broke into the secondary and was racing the sidelines on the other side of the field from me. I crossed the field and saw that I was the lone defender between him and pay dirt. I thought I had a chance to tackle him despite his having one blocker running directly in front of him. His blocker did his job, and down I went, and did not bother to look up. I knew that he scored.

Then I felt the Springhill coaches insulted us by replacing their starting quarterback with the backup. This angered me considerably. It was like saying, "We have you Homer boys beat and we know it." Soon after the replacement came in, he swept right end on a keeper. Nobody blocked me so I had an open-field shot at him. I lowered my head and hit him in the belly with the top of my helmet as hard as I could. He went down and I had a headache. I had forgotten what Glenn Gossett, our new assistant coach, had coached us: when tackling, put your nose on his belt buckle. *The nose, dummy; not the head!*

The only personal head-banging that rivaled this was experienced a year or so earlier when we played Haynesville in Homer. For some reason I had come into the game to replace one of our linebackers on the left side, and Haynesville was driving toward the north goal. Suddenly Haynesville's big fullback, Eugene Ash, burst through the line, running hard. He came straight at me and I made the mistake of hitting him just above the knees. He pumped his knees hard into my face and chin and I held on for dear life, hoping somebody would get there and put an end to this punishment. I felt like a boxer being hammered on the ropes, hoping that bell would soon ring. I was determined not to let go, and I didn't. Finally I had Ash on the ground with me. He popped right up but I was moving like a wounded turtle. Rock Tuggle, who was a tackle on our varsity, was one of the game officials. Along with the stars I was seeing, there was Rock looking down at me, giggling, "Hee, hee, hee. What's the matter, Tabor?"

He thought it was funny.

Springhill beat us by eleven, 31-20, the most points we ever gave up in a single game. In fact, in all of our other five games combined, we gave up a total of 25, an average of five points per game. I suppose the 31 was an anomaly. When we played them again in Homer, they scored just six. The problem was, we scored zero.

Another innovative play that Coach Robinson created at practice was a fake punt that had me lined up as a blocker for the punter. As the ball was snapped I pivoted and ran back behind the kicker as he swung his leg skyward as if punting. The punter handed the ball to me and I ran around left end, hopefully for much yardage, maybe for a score.

We practiced that play a lot and got the timing down, and the night we played Springhill in Homer, I saw a good opportunity to run it. We were behind, 6-0, and had the ball close to midfield on fourth down. Ordinarily players keep their mouths shut unless asked for their opinion. But, thinking that this was a perfect situation and that we may not get the opportunity again I went to Coach Robinson and asked if we could run it. He said no. Instead, we punted. And, unfortunately we lost, 6-0. We practiced that play a lot and never ran it. Never.

Coach Bill Garrett

When Coach May was relieved as head football coach, he seemed to handle the situation with dignity. He continued to coach boys' basketball in 1955–56, and in future years became principal of the elementary school.

Coach Garrett, however, may have felt bitter. He was transferred to Haynesville as a classroom teacher, thus remaining in the parish system. When Coach Robinson's team went there in 1955 to play the Little Wind, as they called their JV team, Garrett was one of the game officials. Robinson had a conflict that night, so Glenn Gossett was our coach. He, of course, had replaced Garrett as assistant football coach at Homer.

During a timeout Garrett strolled over to our huddle and hit tackle Ray Weaver with a heavy insult. "Weaver," he said, his voice dripping with sarcasm, "I thought you were supposed to graduate this year."

No one said anything, including Weaver. Garrett was our former coach, after all. Ray Weaver showed him though. Two years later, as the center for Homer's Iron Men, he made all-state.

Then Garrett targeted me.

One of Haynesville's guards was Paul Brown, who a few years back had moved from Homer to Haynesville. His older twin brothers, Delton and Shelton, had played football for Bill May. I was playing defensive halfback when Paul came downfield and fired a vicious forearm to my jaw and numbed my face with pain. It was totally unnecessary. The running play had ended back at the line of scrimmage. There should have been a major penalty, but nobody made a call.

My face hurt and I was very angry. I quickly became obsessed with seeking revenge against any Haynesville player who got near me. Later, when we were on offense, I saw my chance. During a play I swung my right elbow at a Haynesville player but missed. Garrett saw it. When the play was done, Garrett came at me. He looked me straight in the eye, wagged a forefinger in my face and said, "You do that again, it'll cost you fifteen yards."

A penalty for failure to make contact?

Haynesville seemed to bring out the worst in us. After we tied the score at 6-6, Butch Chadwick went downfield on the ensuing kickoff, and he and I were in on the tackle. After the runner was down I was shocked to see Chadwick begin pounding away with his right fist into the face of the carrier. He didn't get caught, either. I suppose much of this kind of play was part of this game because of the combatants. Haynesville and Homer, thirteen miles apart, were long-time rivals, and we did not like each other. I will say that Haynesville hit harder than any other team I played against. They also played dirtier. And with more tricks up their sleeves.

Insult was added to my injury. Haynesville's running back "Worm" Reeder scored a late touchdown to break the tie and we lost, 13-6. Earlier in the season, on a muddy field, we tied 0-0 n Homer.

Butch Chadwick

Butch Chadwick got into trouble more than the average guy; he seemed to seek it out, thrive on it. He frequently taunted an old man who spent most of his time constructing blowing horns out of cattle horns. The man lived quietly alone in a dilapidated shack near the railroad track, and he did not like to be called Foxy, which of course is what Butch would call him, and then run away. Once Foxy was so enraged he chased Butch into the Pelican Theater.

Another victim was Springhill running back John David Crow, who won the Heisman Trophy at Texas A&M. Crow was a pretty good basketball player, too. In that old cracker-box-like gym in Homer, as Crow sat on the bench during a timeout, Butch calmly walked up to Crow and slapped him on the cheek and then hightailed it to the top of the bleachers. An angry Crow rose from his seat and sought out the offender, but, fortunately for Butch, Crow was persuaded to let it go.

Even I was pushed over the limit by Butch. It was the day I was walking alone just after lunch outside the school on the north side of the gymnasium/ cafeteria. I don't recall the exact nature of my Chadwick-inflicted pain, only that my brain exploded with anger and told me to strike back. The nearest weapon was a wire metal-like container with four equal-sized slots to hold milk bottles. I grabbed it by the handle, and before I could regain my sanity I smacked him hard. The event ended at that point.

The Audis Gill Era

In 1955 I vicariously experienced a measure of revenge against Billy Charles Windsor for knocking the breath out of me. It was the year that Audis Gill replaced May as head football coach. The event took place during an otherwise boring practice on a fall day of that year. We ends were practicing punt return coverage. In this drill a kicker punts the football to a single-file line of running backs waiting down the field. When the ball is kicked, an end runs down the field and attempts to tackle the receiving back, who tries to run the ball back to the kicker. Five or so minutes into the drill end Buddy Pixley got caught at a dangerous place in our single-file line. Buddy and I were about the same size, maybe 130 pounds waterlogged with bricks in our britches. Unfortunately, the back he had "drawn" by random luck to cover was Windsor, whose muscles had recently realized a new growth spurt.

Just before Sammy Camp, who later punted for Tulane University, kicked the ball, I recalled my own experience with Windsor and wondered if Gill knew of May's technique for reviving people unable to draw a breath. I whispered two prayers: one for the health and safety of Buddy Pixley and the other a prayer of gratitude for God's putting me safe behind Buddy in the line.

Camp arched his punt high and long, and Buddy left his spot to run down the field to meet his fate. The rest of us waited for the upcoming crunch and what would be left of Buddy lying in the grass, steamrolled by Windsor.

Windsor caught the punt and started his run. He got nowhere. Pixley hit Windsor at the ankles and leveled him. It was a proud moment for a fellow end.

Pain

There was a lot of pain at Homer High School: the locker room popping of naked buttocks with lethal, wet towels; the hard, open-palm, hand thumps to the side of the head; the behind-the-ear thumps with a flicking of the middle finger from the thumb. Sometimes both types of thumps were executed in one classroom session alone. Often in Algebra II when Mr. Taylor was solving an equation at the blackboard. The usual perpetrator, Ray Weaver; the hapless victim, Archie Snider, who never retaliated.

My threshold for pain was much lower than Archie's. I was minding my own business in the football locker room one afternoon when Red Rock Lindsey, our starting right tackle, using his long, bony, freckled middle finger, flicked said finger from his thumb launching pad, catching the fleshy part of my left earlobe. A wasp sting was a gentle, benign tickle by comparison to the hurt I felt. I literally saw stars. Then Benny ambled away as if the event had not occurred; he stepped on the upright locker room scales and began sliding the rectangular bar to check his weight. Once again, I did not allow sufficient time for my insanity to subside. I reared my right arm back as far as possible and brought my fist down on the middle of Benny's back, creating a dull, hollow sound, which was immediately followed by a little *Uhhh* from Benny's lips. It was a purifying catharsis for me. The insanity left and I waited for Benny to take my life. Not only did he not kill me, he did nothing at all. Just like Butch Chadwick. Butch was bigger than me and Benny was bigger than Butch. Conclusion: right makes might.

When Benny thumped my ear, I had not taken the time to remember his Halloween outing. As older teens we had moved away from simple trick-or-treating to roam the entire town on Halloween night in a number of different groups armed with munitions that would make any military general proud. High-tech artillery like unripe limes. Such projectiles whizzing past your ear at seventy miles per hour made us feel alive. Or possibly dead.

The primary rumor that circulated from group to group one Halloween night was that somewhere across town on the dark streets of Homer, Benny "Red Rock" Lindsey had killed a black guy, possibly with a speeding lime. This bit of news blanketed us with quite a sobering effect. Fooling around with limes is one thing, but actually killing somebody, that's quite a different affair. In those days we had not yet been desensitized by news accounts of drive-by shootings. As a consequence of this fast-moving rumor that was verified by each group that we came across, we decided to put down our weapons, call it a night and go home.

The next morning I got to school earlier than usual to see if Benny would be there or at Angola. I waited at the front of the school along with everyone else. Ten minutes before class the Lindsey Chevrolet, driven by Benny's father, pulled up. Out stepped Benny. He was wearing a white bandage that circled his head just above the ears. What a relief. Our classmate was no longer considered to be a homicidal maniac.

Benny ambled slowly through the quiet hush and broke the silence by chuckling and striking the palm of his left hand with the top of his right, a habit of his. Things were back to normal.

The Tackling Line

The tackling line was a type of physical punishment that our football coaches seemed to thoroughly enjoy. Most likely because they were not in it. They were observers like the Roman citizens who got their kicks watching the gladiators try to calm down those lions.

I qualified for the tackling line because of my love for baseball. I exceeded the football curfew hour by attending a Homer Oilers semi-pro baseball playoff game that went into extra innings. The next day at football practice our assistant coach, Glenn Gossett, told the team that he was at last night's baseball game and that he saw those who broke curfew. The punishment: the dreaded tackling line. Gossett said if the guilty ones did not confess, the punishment would be more severe for them. I thought Gossett was bluffing about being at the game, but I also asked myself if it were possible for Hell to be even worse than it already is. When Bobby Flurry confessed, so did I and a couple of others.

With the tackling line, the chosen "gladiator" is given a football and directed to run over a waiting tackler. Not bad until you consider that this tackler is the first in a single line of others composed of the entire football squad. As soon as the first guy tackles you (or you run over him), you are ordered to immediately get up and go after the next tackler. And the next. And the next....Bear in mind that there are no rest periods.

The tacklers are motivated by the coaches to hit you as hard as possible, not to go easy; otherwise, they become ball carriers themselves. Everybody feared that. Probably even Billy Charles Windsor secretly did. It was not so much the getting hit again and again and again in rapid succession. It was the hellish, end-of-the-rope exhaustion that blanketed you when you still had a ways to go with maybe six or seven awaiting tacklers who had not yet had their moment with you. At this point your supreme exhaustion cries out to you to simply stay on the ground, *no mas, no mas.* Yet you do get up and when you are scarcely off the turf you are immediately hit again, and it seems to be a harder hit than the one before. You get it in your mind that the tackler is a kind of devilish sadist of superhuman strength taking advantage of a sickly, staggering hospital patient trying to rise from his bed of grass, dirt, mud, and tiny bits of laughing gravel.

It is now that strange, guttural moans, with a surreal life of their own, come from you like freight-train sounds of an exorcism. You have actually come to hate the tackler even though he may in the real world, where you no longer exist, be your best friend. And when it is over, and the members of this rite of manhood are leaving the scene of this carnage, you can only lie face down in the gritty grass and allow the necessary minutes for breathable air to return to a normal intake. In time, you will come to know that this experience has made you a stronger athlete and a stronger person who will take on and endure a myriad of yet-born challenges awaiting down the path of life.

More painful than the tackling line but shorter in duration was the belt line. This rite was school-wide, not exclusive to the football team. Those inflicting punishment with this pastime removed their belts and slapped their victims with them as they ran between pairs of sadists strewn double-file down the school grounds like orange cones of caution on highways of disrepair. The major problem with this endeavor is that a few sickos would grab the tail end of their belts and strike their victims with the buckles. Stings a lot but you don't collapse from exhaustion. And if you were lucky, some of the uncoordinated guys would often swing and miss. Of course, you were very motivated to turn yourself into Mercury and run as fast as possible to get to the other end and stop the pain. Why did we do this? Who knows? I think it usually had something to do eighth-grade orientation.

Slickaman Gillaman

Our new head football coach, Audis Gill, had been on the roster as a quarterback at LSU for one year before transferring to the considerably smaller Southeastern Louisiana College in Hammond, Louisiana, fifty-five miles northwest of New Orleans.

His assistant was a young Glenn Gossett, who had been a guard on the Northeastern College football team in Monroe, Louisiana. Gossett's father-in-law was Dave Pearce, who was commissioner of agriculture for the state of Louisiana from 1952–56 and 1960–76. Pearce was also born in Claiborne Parish, of which Homer is the parish seat. When I was writing press releases for the same Southeastern College, I got to be around Pearce in the spring of 1967 when he came to Hammond for its annual strawberry festival. He had a warm, firm handshake, a broad, expansive smile, and a wicked, bad breath.

We football players had known no one else as a head coach except May. So we awaited our new coach with a mixture of curiosity, excitement and nervousness. Gill made a good first impression. He rarely cursed, unless you counted the word *doggone* as cussing. He said *doggone* a lot, often in a cry-baby wail like, "Doggone, I told my wife the night before our game that we were not ready to play." Only it sounded like *dahhg-gun*. Was this guy a Yankee?

Eddie Dewees, who was a junior at the time, soaked up Gill's coaching style and modus operandi: shorter practices than May's and less time spent on conditioning. "I love this coach," Eddie said breathlessly at practice one day. But, in time, Eddie, along with others, became disenchanted with Gill, and the honeymoon ended. Eddie began to make fun of Gill's bald head and called him Slickaman Gillaman behind his back. The creation of Gill's new name probably came about through consultation with the guru of moniker development, Butch Chadwick, who shared Eddie's disdain for Gill. Eventually, they both quit the team.

There was one guy who really liked our new coach. He was the kid who followed Gill to Homer from Forest, Mississippi, in the summer of 1955. Goat, as he was called, suddenly showed up and practiced with us for a couple of days and left quite an impression. He hit people hard and with authority, like a grown man playing with boys. Gill should have known that the Louisiana Athletic Association was not going to allow Goat to live with him and play football out of the young man's home state. After Goat left to return to Mississippi, Gill said to us, "We don't need Goat." It was a lie. With Goat we would have had a very good team rather than a mediocre one.

Gill's signature signoff at the end of his practices was the terse, "That's all." We had not broken the first sweat. And I personally knew I was not at the top of the conditioning chart the night in mid-season when we hosted the North Caddo Rebels. I got tired just warming up before the game.

Gill: Bigger is Better

Where May seemed to favor little guys like Duggo Fincher and Eddie Larkin, Gill thought that bigger was better. After Gill's two-year stay in Homer, he carried that mentality with him when he left in 1957 to be the head coach at Bogalusa, a larger school in south Louisiana. Ten years earlier the Lumberjacks had been state champions. In the fall of 1958 when I was a freshman at Louisiana Tech, a Bogalusa native who stayed in my dorm, showed me a copy of the sports section of *The Bogalusa Daily News*. It listed Gill's starting lineup for an upcoming game. About half the lineup weighed over two-hundred pounds, large for the 1950s. His smallest starter was listed at 179. With this beef, Gill won no games that year.

During spring practice in Homer in 1956, following a workout of little consequence, I sat alone by the game field on the concrete part of the entrance to our dressing room dugout. I was unlacing my high-top leather shoes when Gill approached. Out of nowhere he said to me, "Randall, I should run your skinny little butt off." Because Gill did not push us to get us in top condition, I don't believe he meant to chase me four or five times around the track. He meant that he wanted to get rid of me. Why he wanted this, I have absolutely no idea.

Maybe it was what Larry Andrews had done or not done. I say this because Gill often got the two of us mixed up. His doing that was somewhat understandable because Larry and I were about the same size with similar builds, and we both played end. How I came to play end is a story in itself. During Coach May's tenure I was a halfback, but by the end of Gill's first year in Homer I went to Gill to request a position change. Gill coached the backs, and I wanted to distance myself a bit, so I said I would like to become an end. He was not unhappy with the request. He seemed pleased, in fact. He approved the change immediately without any further discussion, so I left him and the backs on the south side of the practice field and trotted over to Jimmy Bradshaw, who coached ends. Bradshaw, my one-time Sunday school teacher at the First Baptist Church, was a nice guy for a football coach. "I am now an end," I said to him. Then I began to learn a new position.

One day, after I had settled into my new role, we players were in the middle of a scrimmage-like drill that included punting. My side punted the football to halfback Wayne "Bubba" Banks, the fastest athlete on the field. He caught the ball near the old, rusted goal posts on the north end, and I ran down the field to try to tackle him. Banks gave me a head fake to his right and then ran left down the edge of the grass part of the track. I had a good angle on him and a perfect shot. I zeroed in, getting ready to make the hit, when I put on the brakes, slowed down, and allowed Banks to run past me. I did this to save both of us from bodily injury. During his run Bubba had placed himself into what I considered to be harm's way, just a foot or two next to the iron-like beams of the visitors' bleachers, which were supported on the ground by heavy, huge slabs of concrete.

Banks raced the field for a "touchdown" and Gill was livid. Right away, he tore into me with a royal chewing-out. I considered explaining why I had done what I did, but, at the same time, I felt that I should not have to explain the obvious. Besides, Gill, in his state of paroxysm, was in no mood to listen to what he would have surely called "excuses." How would he have reacted if I had followed through? There is absolutely no doubt that Banks and I would have been hurt, maybe badly. Gill would mourn the loss of his star halfback. As for me....

My situation worsened when Larry Andrews screwed up, as we all did from time to time. When the two of us were wearing our helmets I suppose he and I did look much alike. However, invariably it seemed that whenever he screwed up, Gill was quick to assume it was me: "Randall, no, no, no, that's not right..." And the reverse was true. When I did well, I was Larry. When Larry did badly, he was Randall.

On the night of our Purple versus Gold intrasquad game in which we were divided into two teams and played each other, Gill struck again. I had just cut down Billy Boyd with an open-field block he never saw coming. (Billy always claimed that it was a clip, but it wasn't. When he fell, he came tumbling backwards across my body.) And Gill didn't see it as a clip. What he saw was an excellent block by someone else: "Larry! Atta boy! Doggone good block, Larry!"

Lying on the ground tangled up with Boyd, I looked up into the eyes of Audis Gill. He recognized me. "Oh. It's you, Randall."

Fifty-five years later I returned to the scene of my crime on a quiet Saturday afternoon in February of 2011. I stood alone at the spot where I allowed Banks to race past me. The memories came crowding back, and for a moment, I heard Gill's voice, stretched like a tightrope in the air, berating me.

A few things were different. Grass had grown over even more of the old run-down track. And some wise person had made the decision to erect a five-foot chain-link fence to separate the practice field from the blocks of concrete and beams of iron that stood steadfast in the winter sun as if they were awaiting my arrival.

How could I not wonder what might have happened on that long-ago fall afternoon if that fence had been there? Then as I walked away, allowing my mind to comb out those tangles of the past, I realized that I had no regrets. I would do the same thing today that I did in 1956.

The 1956 Season

After our good showing against Jonesboro-Hodge in a jamboree just before the start of the 1956 football season, we players had high hopes for the team. Bubba Banks ran wild in this abbreviated game. As for me, I almost blocked an extra point kick, and I made the tackle on a kickoff, taking down the Tigers' ace back, Johnny Golden. John Wayne Odom finished him off, then jumped up and yelled, "I made the tackle! I made the tackle!" That was okay with me because I was happy, I was having fun, we were winning, and I was excited about the new season. Final score: 19-7.

Our football team opened the 1956 season in Monroe against the Ouachita Parish High School Lions. We moved up and down the field all night long but could score only once and lost 7-6.

The following Monday before practice began, a visibly angry Gill said he wanted to see beneath the south goal posts only those players who had played Friday night, nobody else. When those players grouped at the goal posts Gill ranted and raved and actually used some words considerably nastier than *doggone*. Lucky me. I was spared. I had an exemption.

Gill was so mad he caused a storm system to move into Homer and it rained steadily Tuesday and Wednesday, with Arcadia on the schedule for our next game on Friday. It finally stopped raining on Thursday, which was supposed to be our day for a light practice, wearing our game uniforms, sans helmets and pads. But when we came out of the dressing room two minutes past the scheduled start time, Gill flew into a rage over our tardiness and ordered us back into the dressing room to put our pads on. This we did. Then, wearing our game uniforms, we had a knock-down, drag-out scrimmage in the mud.

Arcadia

The next night when we came onto the field at Arcadia, spectators must have thought that our washing machine had broken. Our uniforms were covered with mud and we had not even kicked off.

I got to play quite a bit and it was fun. Even my failures were. Near the end of the third quarter our quarterback Bobby Flurry called an audible that I didn't hear from my right end position. It was supposed to be a pass over the middle to me. But I didn't run a slant over the middle because I was too busy carrying out my blocking assignment for the play called in the huddle. I had tried once more to block Arcadia's all-state defensive end. I was finding it impossible to drive him from the hole. He was big and he was strong. I did manage to hold him up and thus keep him away from the play so that he didn't make the tackle. But driving him back? Forget it.

When I failed to run my audible pass route, Flurry was sacked for a five-yard loss. We re-huddled and Flurry was not happy. "Randall, when I call out 'blue' and then 'ten' it's an audible pass to you! Be ready. I may call that play again."

He got under center, looked over the defense, and barked, "Team down!" Then he called it. "Blue! Ten! On one! Hut one! On two! Hut two!"

The play failed again. Our timing was off and I had a little rust. I anticipated a high pass, but it came to me low, a little under the knees. We punted, and I zoomed down the field and made the stop on the kick returner. A little consolation. In retrospect, I really believe Bobby Flurry was trying to personally help by providing opportunities for me. He knew me much better than Audis Gill ever tried to know me, ever cared to, for that matter.

We beat Arcadia 28-0 for our first win of the season and the first for Gill since October of 1955. In the dressing room afterwards he was a happy coach. "Doggone," he said, "I don't care who you beat, it feels good to win." (Arcadia was a small school, a classification beneath Homer.) I guess Gill didn't feel very good later on as our disappointing season dragged us through the next three months. We would win only once more. And those 28 points we scored against Arcadia would be the most for us in a single game. Second best was a mere 14 that we scored in a 34-14 loss to Haynesville on a sunny Thanksgiving day. Gill hit a bull's-eye when he said one day late in the season, "Doggone, I told my wife last night that we haven't been able to move the football this whole year."

Losing Gets Old

We lost six of our next eight games and tied one. Most of those games are a blur. When you are losing, the mind seems to bury details of such depressing events into the depths of the subconscious.

After Arcadia, we played our first home game and lost to the Bossier City Bearkats, 35-13, then to Ruston 28-7. Then we beat North Caddo, 13-0. The thing I remember best about that game is getting tired just warming up that humid night before the start. That's when I knew we were not in the best condition we could be. Gill's signature signoff at the end of his practices was the terse, "That's all," when we had not broken the first sweat. I also remember blocking North Caddo's burly left tackle. He was fat around the middle and not terribly aggressive. When I hit him he felt like Jell-O.

The play that stands out in the next game against Springhill is Sammy Camp's punt that was returned to the north end zone for a touchdown. Sammy made no effort to tackle the kick returner. He just watched him run the distance. Camp knew that the score was not going to count because he had just been the victim of a roughing the kicker penalty. The touchdown was erased and we ended up with a 0-0 tie. In those days if a game were tied at the end of regulation play it stayed a tie. It was kinda like that feeling you have when your girlfriend tells you that she likes you a whole lot but she's just not that into you.

The next challenge was Morgan City. This game was a filler, added during the season so we would not have an open date. Before we left Homer on that long bus ride to south Louisiana, Gill told us that we were going to be playing against a bunch of Frenchmen. I wondered why we needed to know this. Were we supposed to play differently against them? Perhaps make adjustments? Brush up on our French? Those Frenchmen turned out to be one point better than us, 14-13. If we couldn't beat our opponents at least we could appreciate their culture.

For the next game we rode the twenty miles to Minden in the individual automobiles of the citizens of Homer. The experience had something like a parade feeling about it. Three or four of us in my group, wearing our helmets and pads, squeezed into one automobile and sat with the ramrod, cramped posture of a British brigadier. When we arrived in Minden, stiff and cramped, but already dressed, we practically stepped from the cars onto the gridiron. At halftime we trailed 14-0, and it ended that way, with no more scoring. Loss number five with two games left.

On a fall morning in the middle of the football season my Dad was driving me to school when we saw Gill about a block from his house, on his way to school like us, except that he was walking and carrying a couple of textbooks just like a student. As Dad and I approached, Gill turned and waved at us for a ride. "Hey, Dad, there's Coach Gill. He needs a ride. Pick him up," I said.

"He can walk for all I care," Dad said with bitterness, and made no effort to slow down. I was starting to feel embarrassed and uncomfortable.

I begged Dad to reconsider; at the last moment before passing Gill by, Dad stopped the car, and Gill climbed in. On the way to school Gill did all the talking. Things like the weather and local politics. Nothing about the subject of football.

One afternoon I ran into Coach May just outside the stadium near the street. He asked me why Gill was not letting me play. I told him that I didn't know. Also I told him that last year before the 1955 season began, Gill said that he was going to take a look at every back, that every back was going to get a chance to run the ball to show what he could do. In fact, equal reps. Not only did I not get the same number of repetitions as the other backs, I didn't get any carries whatsoever.

One student, Glenn Wilkins (brother of Donald and Ray) asked a similar question just outside the cafeteria one afternoon. I didn't have any answers for him either.

When Butch Chadwick quit the football team, he later had some regrets at doing so. I saw him one night at "Teen Town," on the top floor of the Coca-Cola Bottling plant. He and I were shooting pool when he said, "Tabor, I could help the team." I didn't think that he could help that much. Our team needed more than just one additional player. It needed a new G-man.

I refused to let myself take the Butch Chadwick route. Each practice afternoon as we players walked from the school to the football stadium dressing rooms, we passed a raised sign whose words I took to heart: *Winners never quit and quitters never win.* I was not a quitter.

The Homecoming Holocaust

It was homecoming when we hosted the St. John's Blue Flyers, a team everyone, including Gill, expected us to beat handily. After all, St. John's had lost 34-6 to Springhill, a team that we tied, 0-0. Shouldn't that fact make us 28 points better than St. John's?

We had two things here that, mixed together, spelled disaster. One, overconfidence, and two, homecoming. The first curse concerns a coach who takes his opponent too lightly.

The day before the St. John's game Gill called us together following our typical short pre-game practice. He concluded the practice by having specific team members run from the sidelines onto the playing field whenever he yelled out, "Punting team!" "Punt receiving team!" "Kickoff team!" "Kickoff receiving team!" I was hoping he would call out, "Bench warming team!" just so I could race onto the field and feel myself sweat a little.

Once this phase was over, we gathered around Gill to hear his pre-game words of wisdom. He gave us the usual motivational pep stuff and followed that with the kiss of death.

"Tomorrow night I want you starters to get a big early lead so that people like Randall can play." He said the names of other players too, like Pete and Errol and John David but all I heard was mine.

Most coaches know that you never assume, at least in the presence of your players, that you have the game already won before it's played. Both May and Gossett knew doing that increased the risk of your players playing flat. Even against weak teams May cautioned us repeatedly to not take any opponent lightly.

The other ingredient in the poisonous concoction was homecoming. In the fifties it was common practice for the senior players, just before kickoff, to escort homecoming maids from each grade, eighth through twelfth, onto the playing field and gather at the fifty-yard line for official recognition and photographs. Coach May hated this ritual with his guts. He felt that the act of these young ladies holding on to the arms of his players as they strolled from yard line to yard line was a major distraction. He was really big on staying focused on the upcoming game.

Against St. John's we came out overconfident and distracted by all the festivities. And I came out looking forward to playing, as did Pete Moore, Errol Beavers and John David Brantly. Normally we wore gold jerseys, but on that night our male escorts: Wayne "Bubba" Banks, Jerry Lewis, Robby Smith, Bobby Ray DeLoach, Errol Beavers, Billy Boyd, Jerry Crain, and Pete Moore were dressed in white pants and white jerseys with purple numerals. I felt like somebody was about to get married.

St. John's was a team everybody expected us to beat, but those guys from Shreveport came to Homer to play and they played really well. They tackled hard and they tackled well. I sat on the bench and watched us lose, 12-6.

Because one of our running backs had been injured by one of those weaklings from Shreveport, Errol Beavers, a fast athlete whose name was called out along with mine the day before the St. John's game, got his first start ever, against arch rival, Haynesville. I was glad for him; this was his final year.

It was a mild, sunny Thanksgiving day in Haynesville, and Errol played hard but we still lost, 34-14. Season record: two wins, seven losses, and one tie (2-7-1). We scored exactly 100 points in ten games. Over Gill's last sixteen games, his record was 3-12-1. At the end of the school year Gill left Homer to coach at Bogalusa, in south Louisiana. If he had a going-away party, I wasn't invited.

When Gill left Homer I believed that Gossett was the best man to replace him. To me, Gossett was born to be a football coach.

The Glenn Gossett Era

1-AA Track Meet

Shortly before Gill's departure, Gossett was serving as our track coach, not exactly a glamour position. Occasionally assisting Gossett as a volunteer was Mr. Henry Smith, who had a long and illustrious career in education and coaching, and a long life as well (101 years). Mr. Smith taught us how to get out of the starting blocks with quickness.

One day early in the season when the track team was working out in the spring of 1957, Mr. Whatley appeared, striding toward us with purpose and intent, past Mr. Basco's industrial arts building onto our workout site. He had been a track star at Tulane University, where he was known as Rabbit Whatley. We thought he had come to simply watch us practice.

He stopped at the high-jumping pit where I was practicing with a few others. Gossett, who was on the far side of the field, had promised me that if I cleared a prescribed height over the high jumping bar that he would enter me as the No. 2 man in that event. Track and field guidelines allowed a maximum of two entrants from each school in each event.

Mr. Whatley believed in sometimes moving past the boundaries of principalship. We soon discovered that he was on site to teach, to show, to demonstrate, to coach. After a brief greeting, he got down to business, handing me his suit coat, and loosening his tie. "Here's how it's done, boys," he said as he backed up a hasty half-step and trotted confidently toward the bar. All eyes were on Mr. Whatley the high-jumper. All ears too. He jumped. "RIP!"

Mr. Whatley, a well-dressed oak of a man, had done the ultimate for us, sacrificing his suit pants. It didn't seem to matter to him. Without pause or examination of the torn fabric, he continued to teach us. Once he was satisfied with his coaching, he stood before us tall and impressive, his skin glistening with springtime sweat, a loose thatch of wind-caressed hair across his forehead, down to his eyebrows. He brushed back the hair, crammed in the tails of his white dress shirt, straightened his tie, rolled down his sleeves and slipped on his coat. We watched him leave us, carrying himself with stiff, brittle dignity.

Despite Mr. Whatley's expertise, I didn't make it as the No. 2 guy. Doing a practice roll I injured my tailbone landing in the shallow sawdust. A switch to another style of jumping, the scissors, was not successful.

At the Northwestern Relays in Natchitoches, Gossett tried me in the mile. Not enough stamina there. Penciled me in as the No. 2 guy in the 100–yard dash. Fast, but not fast enough. There were faster teammates: Wayne "Bubba" Banks and Errol Beavers.

But Gossett kept tinkering with me and his team until he got it right, finding me a comfortable home in the 880-yard run. Many of us were competing for the first time in some events, but we improved from week to week and meet to meet. *The Prattling Pel* said: "The lack of depth may hurt the Pels, who must take points in every event in order to be a challenger."

At Northwestern, Ray Weaver, high jumping, scored the team's only point. Then at the Fair Park Relays in Shreveport we won 20 points. Haynesville finished first and Fair Park second. Then we showed great improvement by winning 53 points and third place in the annual Haynesville track meet, finishing behind Ruston's defending state champions and second-place Haynesville. Thus, we felt prepared as we headed to the District 1-AA meet in Vivian. The opposition schools, all larger than us, were: defending district champions Bossier City, and Minden, North Caddo, St. John's (Loyola), and Springhill.

We traveled to Vivian in a group of cars rather than a bus. I was fortunate to ride with Mr. Whatley. En route he told some great stories, all better than the pants-tearing story, which he didn't bring up.

We arrived at North Caddo High School early. In fact, school was still in session as Mr. Whatley led us through the main building's quiet interiors. Then the bells rang, and students, in a frenzied disorder, began to change rooms for their next classes. Suddenly I was hit with culture shock: almost all the girls were wearing BLUE JEANS! Clothing that Whatley did not allow for girls back home. They were mandated to wear skirts and dresses, and nobody ever thought to challenge such a rule. Whatley was strict, but he cared about his students, and the impressions they left on people.

Mr. Whatley pulled his mouth in at the corners, held his head back as though sniffing something, and took me gently by the elbow. "Randall, look at how those girls are dressed. Don't you think our girls look nicer?"

His quick question deserved a thoughtful answer. Surrounded by an aura of irresistible femininity, I gazed upon form-fitting jeans and little else. I cleared my teenage throat. "Yes, sir, I sure do," I lied.

I put girls in jeans out of mind and focused on the meet. Outside, the day had begun with an intriguing combination of brisk wind and warm sun that fit together for what I thought was going to be a pleasant spring afternoon. But the weather turned sour, and I could see that we were going to have to squeeze this championship meet in between a few downpours. This meant that we could expect a water-logged track and field.

My event, the 880-yard run, is a half mile, two laps around the track. I would be competing against eleven other runners, including my teammate, Dale "Bird Dog" Bridwell. Five points would be awarded for first place, four points for second, three points for third, two points for fourth, and one point for fifth. Actually ten of us were realistically vying for third place because two guys had a lock on first and second: defending state champion Paul Robinson of Minden, and state runner-up Les Pedron of Springhill.

The gun sounded and the twelve of us were off. The track, which was new, was awful; a reddish pink, sticky, clay-like substance topped the oval, much unlike the hard, black, rock-like cinders that I was used to. As expected, Robinson and Pedron jumped out to an early lead.

About halfway around on the first lap I seemed to hit my stride, running on all eight cylinders. But midway around on the second lap I started to hear my heart pound against my ears. I seemed to slow to the movements of a slug, start to feel a bit feeble. Panic rose, colors exploded in my brain and life went out of me. Fatigue oozed from every pore, and the heaviness in my bursting chest felt like a millstone. My mind kept trying to say things, but my body would not listen. Sections of my body seemed missing, torn away. I was beyond pain; I was simply hanging on for survival.

Nearing the final turn of the last lap, I found myself fifth, hoping to place and earn that point for my team. But I was still moving in slow motion, as if under water. A kid from Bossier by the name of Westerfield was drawing near my right side as the two of us headed for the final stretch to the finish line.

His footsteps grew loud, and he got so close that I could hear his breathing, see his curly blonde hair and his green uniform with BEARKATS stitched across his chest. There seemed to be nothing that I could do to prevent his passing me. The race was lost. I had bombed out.

Suddenly there was Glenn Gossett running along beside us, outside the track. He was frantically making wide, crazy sweeps with his arm. He was in lunatic flight. He was screaming. "Randall! He's going to beat you! He's going to beat you! Come on!"

The tone of alarm in Gossett's furious voice had bite and filled my whole being, bursting magic bubbles in my head, providing a new, electric sparkle of adrenaline. I resurfaced on eight cylinders again, slowly pulled away from Westerfield, increased the distance between us, and crossed the finish line ahead of him.

Panting with exertion I bent forward and grabbed my shaking, wobbly legs just above the knees. The hand of a teammate descended on my shoulder from behind. "Coach said your time was 2:14, Tabor." It would be seven and a half seconds slower than the time of Robinson, who finished first. Pedron was second, just a half second behind Robinson.

From the corner of my eye I saw Gossett. He was calmly entering the results of the 880 onto his clipboard, jotting down my puny one point as if it alone would decide the outcome of the meet. His smug expression revealed an air of conquest. Ignoring me and moving with the hard grace of one who had total control of himself, he walked away to another event. He expected me to beat Westerfield, and willed it to happen. He was not a man who accepted less.

Coach Gossett's track team that could score only one point at Northwestern earlier in the season, won the 1-AA championship easily, compiling 89 points and finishing 25 points ahead of the defending champions, Bossier City. They were followed by Minden with 56, Springhill with 50, North Caddo with 38, and St John's with 2. Homer placed in 16 of 17 events. Gladney Davidson missed getting a point by just one place, finishing sixth in the mile run.

With such a convincing victory perhaps the powers-that-be saw Gossett through the eyes of a 17-year-old: a coach with an incredible energy behind his skills who could extract from his athletes more than they might think is possible, be it track or football. When Gill left Homer, Gossett was named the 1957 Homer football coach, despite the 1956 team winning only two games.

The LHSAA Rules

Before the 1957 football season started, I got the bad news from Mr. Whatley. He had contacted the Louisiana High School Athletic Association about my football eligibility. They declared me ineligible to play for the coming season. Had I been born fifty-nine days later, I would have been okay. The LHSAA has since changed their requirements. By today's rules I would be eligible. The bizarre thing is that some on the team were about my age and they were eligible. I was only two weeks older than halfback Sammy Camp, just three months older than halfback Ray Wilkins, and one month younger than center Ray Weaver. They were all sanctioned to play. If the rule that got me is a bad rule today, then it was a bad rule in 1957.

I knew I would miss being on the field with those guys that I had played with in bygone seasons : Bobby Flurry, G.W. Zachary, Kenneth Hood, Charles Lewis, Jimmy Andrews, Gladney Davidson, John Wayne Odom and Ray Weaver.

Gossett sought me out as I was watching a baseball game on an August evening at the Homer Oilers Baseball Park, home of our semi-pro baseball team. He asked me to join the football team as a manager. I had not considered being a manager in any way until he asked me. I told him that I would think about it. Doing that job would mean putting in long hours of work for an entire football season. I wanted to graduate the following May with a decent academic record, and I knew that having all this extra time after school each day would help me to achieve that goal. I had never before had this much available time in the fall. It was always football.

Before I made my decision I consulted with my friend Peanut Covington. Charles "Peanut" Covington graduated in 1956 and was already attending Louisiana Tech. He encouraged me to take the position. "If you do," he said, "you'll get to stay close to the team."

I considered his thoughts, but I believe one of the main reasons I accepted the job was simply because Gossett had asked. Also, if I couldn't be on the team, then I wanted in whatever way I could to help Coach Gossett in his new adventure as a head football coach.

After I began my duties it was tough, at times, being that close to the guys on the team and not be out on the field with them. However, I stayed so busy and occupied that I didn't have that much time to think about it. Eventually I realized this new experience was good for me in that I wasn't sitting at home every afternoon brooding.

The Birth of Homer's Iron Men

Just before the 1957 season began, somebody approached me at the Purple Cow restaurant one night and sought out my opinion on how good the team would be for the new season. I was not sure. We had lost seven starters, including the quarterback Bobby Ray DeLoach, and the fastest back on the team, Bubba Banks. In the line we lost both starting tackles and both starting ends. I said, "I really don't know how good the line will be, but I think we will have a good backfield." In the backfield we had Bobby Flurry, Ray Wilkins, Sammy Camp, and G.W. Zachary, all good athletes.

Gossett abandoned Gill's belly series that kept us from scoring very much in 1956 and achieved great offensive success. Gossett's offensive coaching style was an interesting blend of conservatism and daring. He knew that when you passed the ball, three things happened, and two of them were bad. Therefore, he did not like to throw the ball much. So it was a conservative but effective ground game. However, if Gossett found his team trailing in a game, he did not hesitate in taking risks, like going for the first down on fourth down and calling for onsides kicks.

The defense was superb. Seven opponents could not score against Gossett's gridders. Four scored just six points. Only Ruston and Morgan City, the eventual state champions, scored more. They were the only two teams to beat Homer that year.

The team, because it was made of a mere twenty players, oftentimes less than that number, became known as the Iron Men, named by *Shreveport Journal* sports writer Jerry Byrd. There is much to say about the Iron Men and the legend they left the town of Homer, but it is simply beyond the scope of this book to do so. The Iron Men deserve a book of their own. Maybe someday someone will write it. Suffice it to say that they went all the way to the state finals that year, but fell to Morgan City, 19-7. After that game when the Iron Men entered a restaurant in south Louisiana for their post-game meal the people from Homer were there to give them and their coaches a standing ovation. It was well deserved.

After they graduated, Flurry, Wilkins, and tackle Fred Miller received football scholarships to LSU, where Miller was an All-American and later played for the Baltimore Colts. Sammy Camp made his way to Tulane and was their punter. Kenneth Hood, John Wayne Odom, and G.W. Zachary played for Northwestern State.

Gill at Bogalusa

1957 Season

When Audis Gill left Homer in 1957, he landed in Bogalusa, Louisiana, about seventy to eighty miles from New Orleans on the north side of Lake Pontchartrain, and two miles west of the state of Mississippi. More than three times the size of Homer, Bogalusa competed in Louisiana's highest football classification at that time, AAA.

In Gill's first season, 1957, he was greeted by a team of thirty-one varsity players, yet Gill told Bogalusa's Quarterback Club that only sixteen of those boys were capable of playing varsity football. That left fifteen to sit on the bench.

The Bogalusa Lumberjacks opened the 1957 season against Warren Easton of Baton Rouge and held a considerable weight advantage, led by John "Jarrin' Jawn" Price, a 215-pound fullback. The other backs weighed from 170 to 190. Three starting linemen were more than 200 pounds. One was 235-pound tackle Dennis Jenkins. For the 1950s these were big boys. Gill's criteria for judging talent had not changed. Bigger was still better.

At Bogalusa Gill must have stayed with the belly series that virtually voided Homer's offense in 1956 because the Lumberjacks failed to score in their first-game loss to Warren Easton, 7-0.

On Sept. 19, 1957, *The Bogalusa Daily News* sports columnist, Lou Major, called Gill's team the "TD Shy 'Jacks." So the next week at practice, Gill ran his running backs down into the end zone "to give them the smell of the goal." Major wrote that Gill was "quite serious about running the backs into the end zone to give them the 'feel' of crossing into paydirt." If Gill had thought of this clever coaching technique in Homer, maybe we could have scored more than 10 points a game. Oh, well, if you can't actually do it, why not go the vicarious route.

In their second game, the Lumberjacks managed to score, but still lost to St. Aloysius, 14-7, a setback that Gill blamed on "bad breaks."

In game three, East Jefferson, a small team, was Bogalusa's Arcadia, and the Lumberjacks beat them easily, 32-0, for Gill's first win since Homer beat North Caddo, 13-0.

The euphoria was short-lived. The 'Jacks next lost to Baton Rouge High, 36-12. Then Gill's gridders went on a three-game winning streak, beating Picayune, Mississippi; DeLaSalle, and Terrebonne. These would be Gill's last wins until 1959.

After Bogalusa could score a total of only six points in the last three games, all losses, Gill told the Quarterback Club that his team was "badly disorganized." This seemed evident in a 7-6 loss to Catholic, in which Gill's players openly squabbled with each other.

Gill must have heard about Coach May's stunt with the Homer basketball team. In Bogalusa's last game of the season against the Bradley Bears of Cleveland, Tennessee, Gill pulled his team off the football field trailing 6-0 with a minute and five seconds left to play.

It seems that Gill was angry about the officiating. When Bogalusa was flagged for roughing the kicker, Gill went onto the field to protest, and when he did, an additional fifteen yards was assessed against his team. At that point he took his team off the field and was soundly booed by the Tennessee fans.

Major wrote that Gill's actions "left a sour taste…in Bradley County after the Lions Club and other citizens had done their best to make the Lumberjacks and their followers welcome."

Gill said the officiating was the worst he had ever seen. "I took so much, but couldn't stomach any more of it. The officiating was awful. There wasn't any use continuing. It just looked like they weren't going to let us play football."

He also accused the officials of being prejudiced and said his boys told him the officials had cursed them. "You know," Gill said, "a coach and a player can lose their tempers sometime, but an official's not supposed to at all."

At the Quarterback Club meeting the following Monday, Gill thanked the citizens of Bogalusa for their "vote-of-confidence" phone calls following the game.

If you discount one loss because of "bad breaks," another for "squabbling and disorganization," and a third for "prejudiced officials," then Gill could have had a winning record of 7-3 instead of a losing record of 4-6. In the next two years, 4-6 would look awfully good.

The 1958 Season

In 1958, Gill's offense scored a whopping grand total of 20 points through ten games, or an average of two points a game. The belly series was alive and well.

The opener was the best game of the season for Gill, a 7-7 tie with small East Jefferson. Then after losing 39-7 to Warren Easton, Gill's team was unable to score a single point over the next seven games. In the last game of the year, facing a season of scoring no more than a total of 14 points, Gill's team experienced the wonderful smell of the end zone by punching across a touchdown in a 13-6 loss to St. Stanislaus.

By the first of October attendance began to dwindle, and Major began referring to Gill simply as "Audis," whereas in 1957 he was respectfully called "Coach Gill." When people quit coming to games, Gill began moving his backs to different positions, making his quarterback a fullback, his fullback a quarterback, etc., and he openly discussed the idea of coaching "from the top," meaning that he was thinking of moving himself to the press box, which he finally decided not to do, because he said his players needed his presence on the field.

On October 20, Major wrote that Bogalusa's "record is about the poorest in the state." Two days later he wrote "the coach of 1959..." (instead of writing "Coach Gill"), also, "The coaching staff still feels the Jacks are going to get high for somebody this season and win a game."

Then the news broke that former Bogalusa coach Arthur "Slick" Morgan, who had gone into private business, had conferred with the school board over the possibility of his return to coaching the Lumberjacks in 1959 because there were reports that Gill did not plan to hold the coaching job then. Morgan indicated that he would replace Gill if the board met his salary demands.

Then Gill told some close associates that reports of his intention to pull out of the coaching picture were "premature and that no definite decision has been made."

Major commented as follows: "When Coach Gill was employed he was recommended to the School Board by a trio of men appointed to screen the applicants. If and when Gill should decide to resign the coaching post, applications would be taken."

Then on October 28, the Quarterback Club gave Gill a unanimous vote of confidence, 22-0. Gill responded by changing his offensive attack to an unsuccessful passing game, led by a converted fullback.

On November 11 Major wrote: "Bogalusa's Lumberjacks this season are having probably the worst time of any team in the school's history in *moving the ball*." (emphasis mine) At a Quarterback Club meeting, Gill was asked why the Lumberjacks always ran the ball up the middle, and never around the end, Gill replied, "We don't have the speed to run wide." No wonder defenses stacked the middle. The team netted a total of 748 yards over the season or an average of about 75 yards a game.

Four of the losses in 1958 were 40-0 shutouts, and three of those were in consecutive order, or a three-game doozy of 120-0. My guess is that four 40-0 losses in a season, with three in a row, is a world's record.

Were Gill's players simply outweighed and outmanned? Hardly. His two starting tackles weighed 200 and 235, his guards weighed 190 and 208, and his center weighed 205. With this beef Gill could not win a single game in 1958. His season record was 0-9-1.

The 1959 Season

Surprisingly, Gill came back for a third season in 1959. After the first game, *The Bogalusa Daily News* headline read: "Jacks Show No Offense in Losing Opener," a 13-0 setback to McComb, Mississippi. Then came losses to Hammond, 20-0; St. Aloysius, 33-6, and Baton Rouge High, 26-6. When Bogalusa finally beat Picayune, 19-0, it marked an end to a seventeen-game losing streak.

On November 22 Major said, "It's the worst two-year record ever turned in by Bogalusa in football."

In three years, from 1957–59, the Bogalusa Lumberjacks never scored against Istrouma, a team that put up 119 points against them in shutouts of 40-0, 40-0, and 39-0.

Gill's three-year record at Bogalusa was 6-23-1. Add in his two years at Homer and it improves to 15-35-2. But if you remove his first year at both schools the record is 4-24-2. Four wins in a three-year period is an average of 1.3 wins a year.

In 1960 Lewis Murray replaced Audis Gill as head football coach at Bogalusa and fans filled the stadium for the opening game, the first time in recent history that the stadium was full.

1957

Warren Easton	0-7
St. Aloysius	7-14
East Jefferson	32-0
Baton Rouge High	12-36
Picayune	32-12
DeLaSalle	7-0
Terrebonne	6-0
Istrouma	0-40
Catholic	6-7
Bradley	0-6

1958

East Jefferson	7-7
Warren Easton	7-39
St. Aloysius	0-21
Baton Rouge High	0-40
Picayune	0-26
Lafayette	0-40
Terrebonne	0-40
Istrouma	0-40
Catholic	0-7
St. Stanislaus	6-13

1959

McComb	0-13
Hammond	0-20
St. Aloysius	6-33
Baton Rouge High	6-26
Picayune	19-0
Lafayette	6-29
Terrebonne	13-33
Istrouma	0-39
Catholic	6-18
St. Stanislaus	20-12

In 1963 Gill returned to haunt me as Barry Morse, who played Lieutenant Philip Gerard, the guy who relentlessly chased David Janssen, a.k.a., Dr. Richard Kimble, in the TV series *The Fugitive*. The resemblance between Gill and Morse was downright spooky. When I first tuned in, for a second I thought Gill, who had fancied himself as a singer as well as a football coach, had decided to try the profession of acting.

Willard the Wizard Returns

I was in high school when Willard the Wizard returned. When he came the first time, his show of magic stunts seemed to have been a financial success because he had large crowds during week nights and full houses on weekends. For a few days after the Willard family had packed up and left, I mourned the loss of Frances, his beautiful daughter, as well as her father and all the magic that he had brought: pulling a white rabbit out of his black top hat, drawing colorful scarves from his tuxedo sleeves, shooting fire from his fingertips, and making money fly out of his hat.

Homer now had television, so I figured those earlier crowd numbers probably would not be replicated. And this time it was a one-night stand and, instead of Willard bringing his big tents, along with Hector and his assistants, he put on his show with just his family members in Homer's spacious city hall, next to where the Pelican Theater used to be. By this time the Pelican was a fire station.

I planned to attend, of course, curious to learn if Frances would still be part of the act. I knew that Glenn Copeland would be there, too, because he loved tricks and magic as much as I did. He was one of the fifteen or so guys in Coach May's commercial geography class. He wasn't a football player; he preferred to spend his spare time refining his talents to become the next wizard. One day he had sat at his desk in the class practicing his craft with a couple of hollow fake walnuts when May discovered Glenn's inattention to the subject of the imports and exports of Brazil. May confiscated the walnuts, opened his desk drawer and placed them inside where they stayed.

From time to time I would ask Glenn if he had gotten his walnuts back. Each time I asked, I received the same response: a sad, slow shaking of his head. The school year ended and the walnuts remained in May's desk. Perhaps May took them home and gave them to his small son, Jon. Maybe there're still in the desk. I'm sure Glenn is wondering too.

At city hall, my seat next to Glenn's was further away from the stage than I preferred but close enough so that I could clearly see Frances when she came onto the stage. I saw right away that she had grown from a child into a lovely woman, Junoesque and goddess-like, bronzed and beautiful. She spilled onto the scene with vigor and grace, and with a toss of her brownish-blonde hair, turned and waved to the audience. Her mother and older sisters came, too, one by one, like flowers rising on their stems at daybreak.

Willard came last, without his cape this time, just a regular dark suit. He seemed older than I expected, not as tall, and there appeared to be some gray in his dark hair. When he pulled out those red, green, blue and yellow scarves, his movements seemed less nimble. Frances, on the other hand, carried herself with a graceful economy and her movements in setting up props for her father were precise, as I fully expected. The family bowed deep before the audience, which politely applauded. The turnout was standard, but not a sellout.

This time I was smart enough to stay put, and not do any volunteering from the audience. Probably Willard would not recognize me after all this time, but there was no guarantee. After all, the man was a wizard. And they say wizards never forget.

At the first call for volunteers, Glenn sprang from his seat as quickly as a ferret and with a nudge here, a hip there, and an occasional light shove, was on stage before I knew it. He was like a rookie quarterback getting his first chance to perform in the NFL. He did admirably alongside Willard and Frances, without any flaws.

When the act was done, Glenn returned to his seat next to me. The first thing he said when he sat down was: "Boy! She is pretty!"

I knew who he was talking about.

Today I know that Frances left the family magic show for a while in the late fifties to be a beauty queen, winning the titles of Miss San Antonio and runner-up Miss Texas. She returned to the group and in the 1960s married a Texas newspaper editor and had three children with him. She became a renowned magician herself and her two daughters followed her into the world of magic and one married a magician. After her divorce, Frances married magician Glenn Falkenstein. They received the Dunninger Award, the Milbourne Christopher Award of Excellence, and were inducted into the Society of American Magicians' Hall of Fame. Falkenstein died on July 4, 2010 of Alzheimer's disease.

Frances and her father, Willard the Wizard, were both born on December 12, she in 1940, he in 1895.

"Ferris" Larkin's Day Off

One of my friends at Homer High School my senior year was Pat Larkin, whose high-boned cheeks and close-cropped, dark brown hair gave him an angular, granite-like, chiseled look. Whenever he placed his lips to the trumpet's mouthpiece to play a solo for Mr. Kendall's band, we listening students who had filled the auditorium knew we were primed for an unforgettable, dynamic experience that would reach into our souls and extract the core fiber of the emotional spectrum.

Pat was our Harry James, standing on his close-to-ground legs on the auditorium stage, pressing down the horn's shiny valves, and tightening the labia of his mouth to hit those elusive, hard high notes. It was a powerful, ultra-pitched, yet mellow sound that made you want to weep through your feelings of melancholy, and at the same time sing out joyous love for the gift of life.

In time, I began to feel that the longer I knew Pat, the less I knew him. He appeared to be weighted down by complex, hidden pressures of conformity that ran contrary to his mild, vulnerable arrogance. His three brothers seemed not to carry this often misunderstood, enigmatic disposition. Eddie, the oldest, had played at a mere 131 pounds the position of center, back when Billy Charles Windsor was running indiscriminately over his own teammates.

Next in age was brother James, whom we usually addressed as "Mug" Larkin. Mug hated country music with an abiding passion. He sneered derisively whenever anyone brought up the likes of Faron Young, Webb Pierce, or the yodeling postman, Slim Whitman, all of whom performed in glittering, spangled, two-pocket cowboy shirts at Shreveport's Saturday night Louisiana Hayride.

The youngest brother was Terry, who was only in the fourth grade when Pat and I were seniors. Therefore, I never got to know him well, but he seemed to be a pleasant little guy who smiled a lot.

Twenty-eight years before moviegoers were introduced to Ferris Bueller, Pat and I took an unplanned, spur-of-the-moment half-day off from school. But instead of using a 1961 Ferrari 250GT California, we made our getaway in my early graduation gift, a 1951 two-door black Ford sedan with Japanese license plates. The previous owner, a military man, apparently had the car shipped home to the states where, through the financial efforts of my parents, I gobbled it up at a Shreveport Texas Street used car lot.

Our act of truancy was totally spontaneous. At some part-way point between the end of Miss Holcomb's first-period senior English and the destination of our next class something convinced us to bring adventure into our day. So, with few words between us, we simply left the building. Outside, the Ford awaited us with a conspiratorial smile beneath its headlights. We got in the car and I started driving, but the Ford took control of the situation and transported us to Minden, twenty miles away, in the next parish.

We ended up at a pool hall and played billiards and snooker and straight pool for the rest of the morning, turning unproductive hours into time well spent. In short, we were blissfully happy and fully alive. By eleven-thirty we became quite hungry but had spent all our money banking shots off the felt-like, cushioned borders of baize. "We'll go to my house," Pat said. "My mother will fix us something to eat."

We returned to Homer and, to my amazement, Mrs. Larkin greeted us with a warm smile and set about making sandwiches, pouring tall glasses of milk, opening bags of chips. It was a simple but delightful meal.

"How will we get back into school?" I asked Pat, wondering why I didn't think of this problem three hours earlier.

"Don't worry. My mom will write us an excuse."

I was surprised by this notion, yet pleased, knowing that my own mother, less than a mile away at that moment, would be firing hundreds of skeptical questions at us and doubting her ethics for even considering such an action.

Minutes later Mrs. Larkin, with a lovely sleepy-cat smile, handed Pat a folded handwritten note like she was passing along a Get-Out-Of-Jail-Free card. I thanked her for making our sandwiches and, our vacation over, we returned to school. I parked with caution in the curved drive in front, where the building's four vertical columns seemed mammoth and more imposing than they did at the time of our departure. I was nervous about pulling off this stunt, but Pat, on the other hand, appeared quite calm, like maybe he had done this countless times. We went into the school office and Pat confidently handed over the note to the secretary and we were welcomed back like prodigal sons.

What was in that note?

Later Jobs

LSU Hill Farm

A job I had when I was in high school was pruning peaches in the spring after school for the LSU Hill Farm Research Station. But everybody, except for those who worked there, called it The Experimental Farm. The peach orchard, located on a high hill off the Minden Highway, was a Louisiana State University test laboratory established to determine growth factors for peaches. LSU hired a lot of boys to thin out the peach trees.

In the spring we workers pruned. In the summer, after the peaches had ripened, we picked them, and LSU sold the peaches to the public. It was a good-paying job and I saved a lot of money.

LSU owned several acres of nearby farmland that were the home for not only fruit trees, but for cows who all day long chewed their cuds and twitched their tag-stapled ears. It was on the narrow, hilly roads of The Experimental Farm that local teenagers did their own experimenting. It was the best nighttime parking and smooching spot in town. They found safety in numbers; a lot of cars, of all makes, models, brands and colors showed up there.

Fulmer's Dry Cleaning

When LSU stopped experimenting with peaches, and my funds began to dwindle, I prayed to find another job. A couple days later a man I did not know called out of the blue and offered me a job delivering dry cleaning out of his place of business. His name was Bert Fulmer and he paid me $30 a week, plus free dry cleaning, except that he meant just the clothes that I wore at work. Those were mostly blue jeans.

There were a few perils attached to this job, namely dogs. Once an aggressive collie tried to bite me as I made a delivery, as well as a German shepherd, but neither of those dogs frightened me like the gang of three

Dobermans that lived at the Hardy house upon a steep hill near the American Legion hut. That trio was flat–out bad, surrounding me and showing off their sharp teeth, all the while growling menacingly. No question. They meant business. I escaped by making circles with my body while swinging the dry cleaning of their owners at them to get them away. As I spun around again and again, I faced each one individually as I got down the hill in circular fashion and into the safety of my delivery truck. I did not complete the delivery that day nor at any time in the future. I suppose the owners of those dogs had to drive in to Fulmer's business place to get their clothes. I really don't know if they did or not because I never asked questions.

The Homer Tobacco

But an unforeseen positive emerged from this employment: my favorite job of all. I believe I would have done this next job for the rest of my life if I could have afforded to. I was hired as a truck driver by the brother-in-law owners of the Homer Tobacco, Candy and Drug Company wholesalers: James D. Kelly and Sidney Cox. Mr. Kelly was married to Mr. Cox's sister.

The job lasted through the summer months and I worked there for four or five summers when I was home from college. My job was to substitute for the regular truck drivers when they took their summer vacations: Butch Crow, Frank Caine, my Uncle Hutto, and Mr. Kelly's nephew, Jack Kelly.

The Homer Tobacco warehouse was a place of immense fun as well as labor. When they were not on the road making sales, Mr. Kelly would bang away at his electric adding machine, and Mr. Cox would direct the rest of us in getting together orders of candy, chewing gum, cigars and cigarettes for the next day's delivery, boxing them, and loading them in the trucks.

I loved the break times, when the entire gang rolled a handful of red dice onto the wooden floor. Whoever rolled the lowest number had to buy for each participant a small bag of Planter's Peanuts and a 6 ½-ounce glass bottle of Coca-Cola. Sometimes we rolled for buttermilk. Somebody there must have had an ulcer. I was low man on the pole; I didn't ask questions. But I did enjoy the buttermilk.

When they discovered that I was a Cleveland Indians baseball fan and that my favorite players were Rocky Colavito and Herb Score, they decided to give me the name *Herb*, or it might on a given day be *Herbie* or even the full *Herb Score*. The name stuck, and Jack was relentless in using it.

Whenever I worked bent over with my back turned, one of those guys would sneak up and goose me in delicate body areas with a wooden box opener, thus producing a variety of strange yelps and cries that even I had never heard. Each goosing event would bring forth collective belly laughs from the others. Two of the men never participated in this sadistic behavior: Mr. J.D. Kelly and Frank Caine. On rare occasions, Uncle Hutto did. Occasionally Butch Crow did. The main sadists were Mr. Cox and Jack Kelly. But it wasn't just me who got it; they goosed each other as well. Like I said, it was a great job.

And it was great being on the road with the guys who taught me the routes: Butch and Hutto and Jack. The rural route was on Monday. It took me through the quiet towns and villages of Athens, Gibsland, Mt. Lebanon, Bryceland, Bienville, Friendship, Lucky, Castor, and Ringgold. In Castor, right by the railroad track, an old and squat pock-faced man had a little store that was unlike any others. I would park in front of his store and leave the bright summer sunshine to enter a small dungeon-like building that was as dark as the Pelican Theater. At some time in the distant past this store must have been a cave. The guy never turned on any lights. His orders were always small and I never saw a customer. Maybe it was a front for a Castor mafioso.

It was in Castor where I experienced my annual August Angst: delivering school supplies for the upcoming school year. The store was Sledge's, the largest business in town. It was across the main street from the local blacksmith shop, where I would sometimes take a break to watch the smithy swing his hammer onto an anvil, and either create or repair iron shoes for horses, and sometimes fit them onto their hooves. It was so fascinating to see this business unfold.

Many stores ordered school supplies, but the granddaddy backbreaker was Sledge's. There was a lot of customer traffic in that large building, so there were frequent interruptions in the process of checking and verifying the order. The regular Sledge orders during the months of May, June, and July were heavy as well, and then when the never-ending cardboard boxes of writing paper, notebook tablets, pens, pencils, index cards, etc. were added on, it was a recipe for a sore back and a test of patience. I guessed this small town must have had one hundred percent student attendance and a teachers' union that dropped the readin' and 'ritmatic and concentrated solely on the writin'.

On Tuesdays I did not have a route. On that day I did an assortment of duties in the warehouse and before it got really hot I walked the cool sidewalks of the Square to the Homer National Bank, where I made money deposits. It was a nice change of pace from the driving days of Monday, Wednesday, Thursday, and Friday.

Wednesdays I journeyed southeast to Ruston, Jonesboro-Hodge, Quitman, and Clay. This was a long route, so I always got an early start by parking my truck at home the night before and departing at daybreak. Ruston, about thirty-five miles southeast of Homer, was the first delivery town, followed by Jonesboro, which was twenty-four miles south of Ruston. By the time I drove into Jonesboro, most people were up and into their day, and certainly all businesses except for one: Traina's Bakery. Mr. Traina never opened before 10 a.m. and many times he fudged on that. I supposed that he was not much of a morning person. Most of the time I simply sat in the truck parked outside the store and waited for his arrival and wondered what he did with his nights at home. Because I was his first visitor each Wednesday morning it would be just the two of us for a while, so we talked uninterrupted until the first customer came in. Mr. Traina's comments led me to conclude that he was indeed a racist. Maybe he was up half the night doing cross burnings.

In Ruston I delivered some huge sealed boxes that, when lifted, felt absolutely empty. A welcomed change from the hernia-inducing school supplies, but on a downside, embarrassment-inducing.. These boxes were not for young students. They were for their mothers. The standard procedure was to take the boxes of the order inside the store, place them out of the way on the floor and then wait until a busy storekeeper had the time to check the accuracy of the order. (It was accurate 99.9 percent of the time.) This checking was executed by the clerk calling out from the invoice the name of each item ordered. As the item name was called, I verified its presence by saying, "check" or "okay."

Some of those folks liked to do it the reverse way, with me calling out and their scanning the boxes on the floor. One of these was a Ruston shopkeeper, a women in her late thirties or early forties. I never got comfortable with the idea of calling out in her presence, names of feminine products, or even the names of those for the other sex, like *Trojan*, for example. At this stage in the checking I could feel my face heat up and my tongue stutter, "one case of *K-K-Ko-...*" The woman who was my partner in this shameful duet was totally nonchalant, totally unfazed, totally patient with my struggle to create words. Once this duty was completed I could relax until the next Wednesday.

It was also in Ruston when I was learning that route under the guidance of Butch Crow that my girlfriend was on the Louisiana Tech campus attending a summer camp of some kind. I had not seen her in more than a week, so I presented a request for Butch to give me a bit of time with her. Butch was a little grumpy about the idea. "We don't have time for that. We have to get back to Homer."

"I promise I'll make it brief, Butch."

"Yeah. I know how it is with you young guys in love. You'll be all day."

Finally Butch relented with a look of doubt about how long this was going to take. He had a thing about time. Each Wednesday he wanted to break his record in the time getting back to Homer. He took pride in that.

I made the visit while Butch sat in the truck. When I returned he looked at me in disbelief. He could not believe that I was back so soon.

"Herbie," he said with a smile, "I believe you could double-park at a whorehouse."

He still had a good shot at breaking that record.

Thursday was the route to the big places: Minden and Bossier City. The smaller of the two trucks was used for this route and there would be no extra space for anything.

Friday was the East Route which included the towns of Bernice, Lillie, Spearsville, Marion, Linville, Farmerville, and Haile. Jack Kelly figured I had never heard of a place like Haile, and he was right. The first time he took me on this trip to learn the route he said, "Herbie, today you're going to Haile." I had never been there, of course, and when I did get there, it wasn't very much. Just a couple of stores.

Later, as Jack drove about halfway between Farmerville and Bernice, and I sat in the passenger seat trying hard to remember all the turns, stops, and landmarks, he seemed to be thinking about something. He grinned and said, "Randall, I'm going to give you some education. Women like it as much as we do."

"Like what?"

Jack looked at me like I was Moe Stooge, then continued. "Yes, sir, they like it as much as we do. Don't think otherwise."

I decided that he did not mean baseball. "That's good to know, Jack."

Years back he must have shared his valuable information with that drunk at Taylor's Drive-In.

"AP What?"

From 1955 through the following years I felt I knew each Cleveland Indians team as well as any other rabid fan. But that alone would, of course, not get me hired to manage them. Had I sent a letter of application for a managership, explaining my loyalty and knowledge, it would have gone into the rejection bin. Even if I my letter had offered my managerial genius for no salary, instead just a season's supply of chewing tobacco. (In baseball it's important to be one of the guys.)

So in the late fifties I took the vicarious route. Perusing a baseball magazine in my parents' living room one evening I spied an interesting advertisement from the APBA Game Company. For about $20 plus shipping, I could actually manage the Indians to a world's championship, in the realm of make-believe. The magazine hype really dazzled me, so I sent my money to Lancaster, Pennsylvania, and two weeks later a blue and white cardboard box the size of an extra-large pizza arrived.

It was a neat, exciting game. Not only did it replicate the past season's statistics of each team in both the American and National leagues, it had some nice extras: balks, steals, players who ran into each other and got injured, others who got ejected for arguing with umpires, pitchers throwing so well that they became stronger as the game progressed into the late innings. And sometimes it rained. Rainouts were rare. Only once did I ever roll the dice, check the player card, and appropriate chart and read: *Game called because of rain.* Playing this game was like being at Municipal Stadium in Ohio.

Along about this time Bob Haley and I were attending Louisiana Tech. He had let me know that he was a long-time Detroit Tigers fan. Bingo! I had found a player partner.

When we were home for the summer, on balmy, sunny afternoons I would take my game box, along with its contents of numerous boards, charts, dice, and player cards to Bob's house in Homer and have a showdown with those Tigers and the card that represented their star player, Al Kaline. And there were refreshments in Briggs-Haley Stadium. Somewhere in the middle innings, Bob's mother, Gladys, would come into the living room where our game was in progress and serve the managers tall glasses of iced tea or cold lemonade.

A little later on I ordered another APBA product: the NFL football game, whose box was identical to the other, except that it was red and white. Inside were the expected boards, charts, dice, and player cards.

My new opponent was Butch Fincher. When he and I met on our mythical gridiron he coached the Baltimore Colts, who had won the NFL championship the season before, and I chose to coach the New York Giants. These teams in real life had battled in that historic game that turned the corner for professional football. Millions had watched on black and white television as Alan "The Horse" Ameche plunged into the end zone for Baltimore's overtime win.

Butch and I re-created this memorable contest at least a dozen times with about an even split. Both teams scored a lot of points. The game was so realistic it allowed us the luxury of keying on individual players and Butch did just that, his primary target being Frank Gifford. Coach Tabor's big worry was figuring out how to stop Johnny Unitas.

Most often we played on cold winter afternoons in the den of his in-laws, Mr. and Mrs. Cortez Bays, who lived out past the high school on the oilfield road.

One other participant shared in this joy, Uncle Hutto, who never met a game that he didn't like. He and I played both of the APBA products.

These games provided the four of us with countless hours of pleasure, and today there are times on summer afternoons and winter evenings when I would give anything to be sitting across from one of these friendly foes, trying my best to outguess, outmaneuver, and outscore him.

My Gridiron Uncles who played for the Homer Pelicans: (from left) Elton Tabor, class of 1939; Hutto Tabor, class of 1948; and Dude Tabor, class of 1943 (Homer High School Collection)

As evidenced here, Dad, although serving his country
well, did not seem to care for the Army. Mom appears
to share those feelings. (J.R. Tabor Collection)

At the center of the town a rainbow of lights were strung from the top of
the courthouse to the buildings across the streets, turning the Square
into a breathtaking, mountainous carousel. (J.R. Tabor Collection)

Mr. L.R. Tanner, principal of Homer Elementary for
twenty-one years (Homer High School Collection)

Miss Evelyn Holcomb, English teacher (Homer High School Collection)

Mr. Phillip B. Kendall, band director (Homer High School Collection)

Mr. H.W. Whatley, principal (Homer High School Collection)

The birthplace of my infamous nickname, "The Amber Inn
Kid," is the Amber Inn restaurant in Bossier City, La. The
twenty-cent milk shake is what did me in. These carhops were
not on duty that fateful night. (photo, Jack Barham Collection,
LSU-Shreveport Archives and Special Collections)

Standing (from left): Billy "Smut" Smith, Brice Causey,
Johnny Ebarb. Kneeling (from left): Louis Bufkin,
Richard McComic (Homer High School Collection)

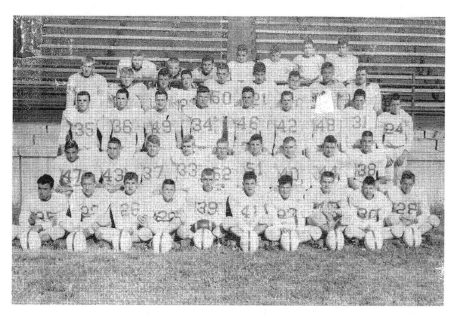

Coach Bill May's last Homer football team (1954). Front Row (from left): Errol Beavers, Benny "Red Rock" Lindsey, Fred Miller, John David "Wombat" Brantly, Ted Maddry, Raymond Hollenshead, John David "Shoes" Mitchell, Theron "Pete" Moore, Jackie "Squirrel" Brantly, Jerry Crain. Second Row (from left): Albert Green, Alan "Rock" Tuggle, Joe Simpson, Charles "Peanut" Covington, Byron Ruple, Bobby Joe Edmonds, Hodric Caskey, Jerry Lewis, Robby Smith. Third Row (from left): Bobby Ray DeLoach, Wayne "Bubba" Banks, James Banks, Billy Boyd, Gene Hammontree, Billy Charles Windsor, unidentified, Ray Wilkins, Bobby Flurry. Fourth Row (from left): David Tooke, John Wayne "Rollo" Odom, Gladney "Satch" Davidson, John Randall Tabor a.k.a. "The Amber Inn Kid," Sammy Camp, Phillip "Butch" Chadwick, Eddie Dewees, Herman Coleman, Terry "Buck" Tuggle. Back Row (from left): Harry Shackelford, Kenneth Hood, Larry Andrews, Deryl Ackley, Philip "Butch" Fincher, Charles Lewis, Eugene "Buddy" Pixley (Homer High School Collection)

Coach Bill May removed his team from the Junction City gym in the middle of a game when he thought he was getting a raw deal from the officials. Standing (from left): Sammy Camp, Ray Weaver, Bob Haley, Benny "Red Rock" Lindsey, Robby Smith, Bobby Flurry, Fred Miller. Kneeling (from left): Philip "Butch" Fincher, Sammy "MacBeth" Simpson, Ray Wilkins, John David Brantly, Coach Bill May (Homer High School Collection)

Cheerleaders for 1954: Eddie Simpson, Kay McFarland, Marilyn Brown and John William "Squealer" King (Homer High School Collection)

At the left edge of these bleachers is the area where I allowed Bubba Banks to run free. (photo courtesy of Beverly Smith)

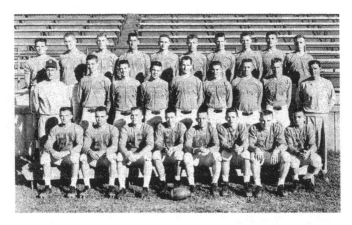

Audis Gill's last Homer football team (1956) First Row (from left):
Pete Moore, Errol Beavers, Bobby Ray DeLoach, Randall Tabor, G.W.
Zachary, Charles Lewis, Kenneth Hood, Deryl Ackley. Second Row
(from left): Coach Gill, Edward Ellis, Gladney Davidson, John D.
Brantly, Wayne Banks, Larry Andrews, Jerry Crain, Huey Wallace,
Coach Gossett. Third Row (from left): Ray Wilkins, Benny Lindsey,
Billy Boyd, Robby Smith, Jerry Lewis, Herman Coleman, Bobby Flurry,
Ray Weaver, Fred Miller, Sammy Camp.(Homer High School Collection)

Pat Larkin was voted best musician at Homer High
School. (Homer High School Collection)

Homer High School in the Fifties (Homer High School Collection)

Like Father, like daughter, like granddaughter, we seem to share
an innate love for our dogs. (from left): Me with Dan, Leigh-Ann
with Charlie, and Anna with Buddy (J.R. Tabor Collection)

The Indefatigable Danny Walker (right): shows colleague
Dr. Vincent Marsala (now LSUS chancellor) the grip that
enabled him and his partner to win the LSUS mixed–
doubles tennis championship. (photo by J.R. Tabor)

(from left): Dad, Mom, Aunt Gladys and Uncle Tommy share a laugh
about Dad's intimidation of a group of foul-mouths. (photo by J.R. Tabor)

Here Grandson Bailey Tabor, the Rebel in Tiger Stripes, is absorbed in the play of his favorite football team, the LSU Tigers. Little sister, Riley is absorbed in a bug on the floor.(photo by J.R. Tabor)

Heisman trophy winner Billy Cannon autographs a picture for Bailey Tabor. (photo by Cheryl Moss)

Joe Michael (far right) wasn't in the suit-selling business as much as the suit-fitting business. With Joe are (from left): Mrs. John Randall Tabor (Carolyn), Mrs. Dude Tabor (Margaret), and Mrs. Joe Michael. (photo by J.R. Tabor)

Governor Edwin Edwards promises LSU-Shreveport a new parking area, concrete included. (photo by J.R. Tabor).

The Tabor Pocketknife passes from C.L. to me, to
Jonathan, to Bailey. (J.R. Tabor Collection)

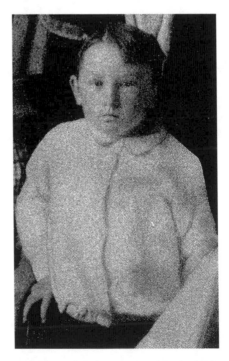

Dad was almost fourteen years old when the stock
market crashed in 1929. (J.R. Tabor Collection)

Diversity at its best: The Friday Pizza Bunch. (*home areas in parentheses) Seated (from left): Dr. LaWanda Blakeney (Alabama), LSUS music professor; Dr. Ernie Blakeney (Alabama), Centenary College professor of chemistry; Chris Nolan (Florida), professional creative photographer. Standing (from left): Ron Sereg (Iowa), LSUS professor of public relations; Frank Bright (Louisiana), Shreveport attorney, retired; John Randall Tabor (Louisiana), LSUS professor of mass communications, retired; Carolyn Tabor (Louisiana), professional caretaker; Melly Sereg (Panama), librarian at Shreve-Memorial Library; Dr. Jack Nolan (New York), LSUS professor of mass communications, retired; Suzzanne Bright (West Virginia), LSUS professor of mass communications, retired (photo by Ron Sereg)

Here, I'm pinning a corsage on Mom. I am a better person today because of my mother. (J.R. Tabor Collection)

George McCalman fires a corkball as his brother David gets ready to make the catch (photo by J.R. Tabor)

Dad at the controls. When he was forty-seven Dad and I worked on an oil rig much like this one. (J.R. Tabor Collection)

Charter members of the Mortimer Adler Philosophical Society (MAPS) (from left): John Turner, John Randall Tabor, Pat Turnley (Photo by J.R. Tabor)

Part II

> When I was a child, I spoke as a child, I understood as a child, I thought as a child: but when I became a man, I put away childish things.
>
> 1 Corinthians 13:11

One Sneeze is Worth a Thousand Colds

When I was an undergraduate at Louisiana Tech my popularity rating vacillated as much as that of a United States president. Most days I experienced less than widespread acceptance. But on Fridays, when the Tech dining hall served its noontime fried shrimp, my approval rating shot into the stratosphere because I did not like fried shrimp and every one of my Homer friends did, namely Bob Haley, Butch Fincher, Tommy McCalman, Buddy Pixley, John David Brantly, and Kenneth Gordon.

Mondays through Thursdays I was virtually ignored. But as the Friday clock ticked closer to noon, the buttering-up began. It was a fierce competition. As we walked from our dormitory, Hale Hall, to the dining facility, those aforementioned friends jockeyed for position to walk next to me and drape a palsy-walsy, fraternal arm over my shoulder in hopes that my serving of shrimp would soon find a home in their stomachs.

Inside the dining hall, it got shamefully worse. I felt like the belle of the ball as hungry Homerites attempted to determine the table I would take my food tray to. The moment I sat down, the seats in close proximity would be quickly claimed.

I don't recall the criteria in choosing the fortunate winner. All of them had nice things to say about me (Randall, ol' buddy), but I had the feeling they were more interested in getting to know my shrimp rather than getting to know me as a person.

There were other dining hall experiences.

One day, standing in line to pick up a food tray, I just missed by inches getting my shoe tops decorated by an unfortunate girl who threw up just in front of me. Suddenly already bad college food joined forces with the rancid stench of vomit. I returned to Hale Hall, plopped into bed , and, with a devouring gulf of despair, listened to the grumbling sounds of my stomach for the rest of the day.

Then there was the time that my "fair weather" friends and I sat at a dining hall table plenty big to oblige the whole bunch of us. It was a very cozy arrangement, made even cozier by the fact that all the tables of the dining hall were placed quite close together, apparently to accommodate as many of Tech's 3,900 students as possible.

At our table I sat on the northwest corner to the right of McCalman and Brantly. Directly across were Fincher, Haley, and Pixley. On the far end, Gordon. This arrangement put me so close to the girl sitting on the northeast corner of the next table that I could have reached over and patted her left shoulder.

Suddenly in mid-bite I noticed a quick movement from the girl. She turned to me and emitted a gale-like sneeze that rocked my chair. Following a half second of stunned silence the occupants of my table roared in laughter, led by the booming guffaws of one Bob Haley.

Poor girl. Poor me. Another appetite killer.

Dog Days: The Tech Era

W hen one speaks of dogs and Louisiana Tech University in one breath, usually it is an association with the college's antediluvian mascot, the bulldog. Although the following three dog tales have nothing to do with that breed, they do connect with my time as a Tech undergraduate from 1958–62.

And although dogs had been the farthest thing from my freshman mind in 1958, two of them in particular easily captivated my attention as well as that of other Techsters as we walked across campus one Monday morning on the way to class. Me, I was diligently headed to Professor John Winters' History 401. On all other campuses throughout the land this course would have been History 101. Since I didn't ask, I never knew why Tech's freshman classes were classified at the 400 level. But the numerical analysis of academic offering did not concern me at the moment. What did was the two canines engaging in whoopee halfway between the campus bookstore and Keeney Hall.

Even we students from small towns like Homer knew enough to cast only furtive, oblique, half-shy glances at the romance in progress. All of us except for one wide-eyed coed who must have led a totally sheltered existence back home in Dubach or Hico or wherever. With books in arms she stood transfixed, stone-like, mouth agape, openly observing the hanky-panky with a startled-fawn expression.

The passersby smiled at her in a controlled, mirthful way and choked back their laughter. But she was completely oblivious to them. Only the dogs held her attention. I moved on to class, leaving her standing there like a frozen post.

Fifty minutes later I strolled out of history on my way to my next class. The mesmerized coed had thawed out, I guess, and was nowhere to be seen. As for the two lovers, they were relaxing under an oak tree enjoying what appeared to be a cigarette? No, not at all. It was a small white bone they were sharing.

The Tech dormitory room (222) that I shared with Tommy McCalman and John David Brantly in Hale Hall had been christened as The Three Deuces Bar & Grill by its former inhabitants. Down the hall and around the corner was the room of Bob Haley and Butch Fincher. On the same floor in close proximity to them Buddy Pixley and Kenneth Gordon were roomies.

At some point during the semester the locking mechanism for the door to Buddy and Kenneth's room became defective. If you jiggled the knob of their locked door just right it was like saying, "Open Sesame." Anyone who knew about this had access at any time.

One pleasant afternoon John David and I were returning to Hale Hall after getting out of zoology lab early. Just past the home economics cottage we saw a friendly tan dog whose acquaintance we quickly made. I don't remember who thought of it first, but together we came to believe that Buddy and Kenneth, who we knew were in class at the time, should have the opportunity to bond with our new four-legged friend.

It was easy to coax the dog to come along with us to the dorm. Once there, and after a few jiggles of the door handle of the Pixley-Gordon abode, we introduced the dog to his new quarters. After making sure he was comfortable we closed the door and hightailed it to The Three Deuces before anyone saw us.

This must be said: Buddy and Kenneth were very good sports about the practical joke. Obviously they were well aware of the cardinal rule of being a college freshman: all's fair in innocent prankage. Whatever happened in that room after John David and I left was never mentioned. Don't ask; don't tell.

Later as an upperclassman in the early sixties I no longer spent every weekend in Homer. Staying in Ruston most weekends led to the problem with Bimbo, a misnamed pup if there ever was one.

Along about the time I enrolled in Tech as a freshman, Dad's work took him away from home nights, leaving Mom all alone except for Dan, the German shorthaired pointer. To provide protection and company for her in his absence Dad went out and bought her a full–blooded Chow-Chow for $15. Since the dog was owned one hundred percent by Mom, she, unfortunately, had naming rights. The name she picked went way past the boundaries of irony. Dad must have cringed inside as I did when Mom said to us one day in the living room: "His name is Bimbo." I was hoping for something like Stalin or Satan.

Despite the name, Bimbo had incredible genes as well as loyalty and manners. Whenever I gave Dan and fully grown Bimbo their daily food rations I simply mixed their grub in one large container and divided up equal portions into their two bowls. Because Dan was always in such a starvation frenzy at dinner time, I fed him first. As his share tumbled into the bowl he gobbled with rapid, huge bites.

Then it was Bimbo's turn. What a contrast between two members of the same species. Bimbo stood back and watched as I scooped out his half. When I finished, he took another half step back and looked up at me as if to ask, "Sir, is it permissible to dine now?" After my tacit approval only then did he begin to dine, eating slowly.

Of course by this time Dan was done. And after he was done he inched his nose into the area of Bimbo's bowl. Whenever that territorial transgression occurred, Bimbo, without raising his head, stopped eating and emitted a low, serious growl, showing a few sharp teeth for extra effect. Dan was smart enough to back off.

Others backed off too, like delivery boys and mailmen and meter readers, all of whom Bimbo kept in a paroxysm of fear by his presence. As far as I know, Bimbo never bit a human. But humans were so intimidated by him they were not about to come into the yard and go into the record book as being the first bitee. They could not believe what they were hearing when Mom came out, and with a sweet edge to her singsong voice, cooed, "Now, Bimbo, be nice,."

Bimbo was not perfect. As I stayed in Ruston more and more I guess he forgot me. One Saturday in the early sixties I pulled into the family driveway, and as I got out of my car, was shocked when Bimbo began barking at me non-stop. I think I was a little heartbroken. But I realized that he was simply protecting Mom, which he did daily until his death a few years later. But before that time came, he and I got to know each other again, and he never barked at me after that.

Link's Elhew Raider

Before Dagwood there was Raider, who had followed Freckles and J.R. in my friend Conway Link's succession of German shorthaired pointers. Full-blooded and registered, Raider carried the official name of Link's Elhew Raider. But sometimes Conway called him Raider of the Lost Bark

Raider was the only dog I know that had his own major credit card. This became a reality when his owner/guardian Conway sat down at his desk one day and filled out several credit card applications in Raider's name. Mastercard, Visa, Montgomery Ward, Penney's. I got drawn into this bit of lunacy a week or so later when I received a phone call from a very nice lady from JCPenney Life Insurance Company, who, since I apparently had been listed as something of a personal reference, had a few questions about Mr. Raider. This took place in the eighties, so I don't remember her specific queries or all my answers, but I believe that she must have misread "pointer" in the application form's occupation blank to be "painter." Whether she pictured Mr., Raider as the latest Michelangelo or somebody like a regular house painter, I do not know.

Anyway, I spilled the beans by asking, "Are you aware that Mr. Raider is a dog?"

After a few seconds of silence the nice lady seemed to become a bit flustered. "Mr. Tabor, " she said as kindly as possible under the circumstances, "we do not insure dogs."

Penney's rejection was one of many that came back from the twenty to thirty businesses that received Raider's applications for credit cards, life insurance, and who knows what else.

About a month later I ran into Conway. He wore a huge grin. "John, we have happy news."

"What news might that be, and who is *we*?" I asked.

"My beloved son Raider and I."

Without further words, Conway whipped out his wallet and extracted a brand new credit card. On the card's surface were the raised capital letters that spelled out: LINKS ELHEW RAIDER.

Somewhere deep within my sense of justice and accountability I felt that Conway needed to pay the full price, whatever that might be, for hoodwinking Mastercard. It should cost to skate so close to the lunatic fringe. The next time we had lunch, I urged him to charge our meals with Raider's credit card. He wouldn't do it.

I tried to appeal to his sense of unreasoning. "Conway, what if Raider ever wanted to move out of that thing you call a doghouse and buy himself a *real* home? He would need a credit history in order to apply for the mortgage loan."

It didn't work. No amount of pressure could persuade him.

Thus, a few years later Raider passed away without ever experiencing that delusional joy of postponing payment for a product or service as you and I do on a monthly basis. To be a fair-play "father," Conway must not favor one "son" over another. I say, "Cards for Dagwood and Bay Leaf!"

— Give Your Heart to a Dog to Tear —

Sometimes I think I like dogs better than humans. Awhile back as I was mowing my yard in rural Bethany, I glanced up from my cutting pattern to see a white van pull up in the cul-de-sac. An occupant of the van proceeded to let out two rottweiler pups.

Before I realized that an act of canine abandonment was taking place ,the driver of the vehicle sped away with the pups in pursuit. In seconds they gave up the chase and trotted slowly over to my vicinity. I stopped the mower, squatted, and extended a gloved hand. The bigger of the two cautiously came over and allowed me to rub his furry head. When the smaller one finally came near with its feeble cough, I realized they were sick pups.

Minutes later, a neighbor from down the street came by to tell me that he too had seen the despicable act and intended to call the pound. Neither of us got the van's license plate number. My neighbor said that as the inhumane person drove past his house, the driver covered the side of his face with his left hand.

A little later I noticed that the pups were nowhere around. Something told me that I might find them in my open garage. My intuitive guess was correct. They were huddled deep in the garage, right at the door leading into the house.

I pondered about the kind of person who would abuse helpless animals like the pups. Historically, man has always been inhumane to his fellow man. We see that a lot in the Old Testament. And man has always attempted to offer excuses for his inhumanity. In some warped, weird, psychotic way he has repeatedly offered lame justification for the torture and murder of fellow human beings.

But how can he excuse the abuse and abandonment of the defenseless, those long rumored to be our best friends? Cruelty to those who have never started a war or enslaved their own species?

The aggressive acts of dogs are instinctive. One might also make this argument on behalf of Homo sapiens except for the fact that most humans can reason.

Leaving my half–mowed yard, I marched inside and punched in the phone number of *The (*Shreveport) *Times*' "Tell-the-Times" and yelled into the mouthpiece: "to the people who stopped their white van on our dead end street in Bethany and abandoned two sick rottweiler puppies, all I can say is shame on you!"

Dogs are so loyal and loving. When your day is terrible, when you've lost your wallet, when your boss chews you out, when you've struck out twice in a softball game, those loving licks from big, wet tongues and sorrowful looks of sympathy make things immeasurably better.

From my first dog, Shorty, through Dan and Hiber and Bimbo, and the labs Lainie and Old Black Joe, to my present Hannah, I have loved dogs. Loved them because when they chose me as much as I chose them, they made life beautiful. And today it seems that inclination has passed on to my daughter Leigh–Ann and her daughter Anna. Their love for Buddy is unconditional.

In the 1960s I wrote a short story about my dog that was killed in the early 1950s by a speeding delivery truck driver who deliberately swerved into him. The title of the story, *Give Your Heart to a Dog to Tear*, was taken from the Rudyard Kipling poem, *The Power of the Dog*. The fourth of six stanzas from that poem follows:

When the body that lived at your single will,
With its whimper of welcome, is stilled (how still!)
When the spirit has answered your every mood
> *Is gone —wherever it goes—for good,*
> *You will discover how much you care,*
> *And will give your heart to a dog to tear.*

Another great dog poem, *The Rainbow Bridge*, was inspired by a Norse legend. The author is unknown. Here it is, in full:

By the edge of a woods, at the foot of a hill,
Is a lush, green meadow where time stands still.
Where the friends of man and woman do run,
When their time on earth is over and done.

For here, between this world and the next,
Is a place where each beloved creature finds rest.
On this golden land, they wait and they play,
Till the Rainbow Bridge they cross over one day.

No more do they suffer, in pain or in sadness,
For here they are whole, their lives filled with gladness.
Their limbs are restored, their health renewed,
Their bodies have healed, with strength imbued.

They romp through the grass, without even a care,
Until one day they start, and sniff at the air.
All ears prick forward, eyes dart front and back,
Then all of a sudden, one breaks from the pack.

For just at that instant, their eyes have met;
Together again, both person and pet.
So they run to each other, these friends from long past,
The time of their parting is over at last.

The sadness they felt while they were apart,
Has turned into joy once more in each heart.
They embrace with a love that will last forever,
And then, side-by-side, they cross over together.

Long, long ago, when man and dog realized they needed each other to produce hunts of success, they bonded and shared in the quest for game and its mutual enjoyment around primitive campfires. That symbiotic relationship miraculously continues to this day, despite man's inhumanity to his four-legged friend.

— The Indefatigable Danny Walker —

D anny Walker did more in a day than most people do in lifetime.
A graduate of Shreveport's Fair Park High School and later
Northwestern State in the 1960s, Danny wore a multitude of hats
and he wore them often. While pretending to be a sociology professor at
LSU-Shreveport he was also co-owner of an upscale Mexican restaurant in
St. Vincent's Mall,

a member of a touring softball team that traveled as far away as Missouri
on weeknights,

a much–in–demand speaker about President John Kennedy's death.
(Shortly after the assassination Danny had somehow acquired a copy of the
original Abraham Zapruder film, one of the most important documents of
the 20th century. In showing the film repeatedly to various groups, Danny
became something of an expert on the topic.)

a qualified Methodist minister whose dirty jokes were second to none,

a standup comic who masqueraded as a commencement speaker for
school graduations,

a radio sports announcer who did the unexpected on the air.

It was during the 1970s when Danny pulled his famous broadcast
stunt. I had invited him to a Friday night party at my home in Broadmoor
Terrace, but Danny, as usual, had a conflict: he was to be the play-by-play
announcer of an end-of-the season football game between winless Booker
T. Washington High School and winless Green Oaks High School. He
declared that he would come to the party right after his broadcast duties
were done, but made me promise to turn on the second half of his game and
have the partygoers listen. He guaranteed something special.

We knew Danny would not fail us, so we tuned in and listened. Following
an uneventful third quarter, Danny went into action in the fourth. Something
like this came from the radio:

"John Tabor goes crashing through the Green Oaks line for a fifteen-
yard gain.

"A crushing tackle made by safety Jimmy Bates. Bates, a transfer student from Homer, has played the game of his life tonight."

Danny took care of us Homerites right away, then moved on to describe the heroics of Professor Bill Scott, Professor Charles Johnson, Professor Conway Link, only Danny called them fullbacks and tackles and guards. His partner in the broadcast booth kept saying, "I don't see those names on my roster..." Undaunted, Danny continued on, keeping us in the heat of the gridiron battle, describing with gusto, our runs and tackles and blocks and throws and catches. By the end of the game, we were exhausted.

When Danny arrived at my house after the game he of course, ate up all the attention he got.

As I write about Danny I close my eyes and try hard to visualize Danny in the state of sleep. I am not able to do so. Perhaps no one has ever seen him in such a state, for there is a rumor that he never sleeps. His daily twenty-four hours he spends in motion, arms, legs, head, mouth, especially the mouth.

Relatively short and stocky and blond, Danny mastered many sports at Fair Park: baseball, basketball, tennis, golf. His best was probably tennis. Unfortunately, I happened to meet up with Danny in a mixed doubles tournament on the tennis courts of LSUS, where we were on the faculty. Although his physical skills were plenty enough to win the match for his side, Danny took no chances. During our match he raced about the court, this way, that way, to the net, from the net, his mouth moving at the same rapid pace; he was constantly singing made-up songs, reciting poems and jingles, posing riddles, telling jokes, making friendly insults, all during lobs, smashes, backhands, serves, all non-stop. Make no mistake. It was quite distracting. Yes, my side lost. In fact, Danny and his partner were tournament champions.

A small measure of revenge came my way later on the links of spacious Huntington Golf Club in Shreveport, where Danny and I and two other NSU grads grouped as a foursome one day. Charlie Johnson (a Fair Park alum and LSUS mathematics professor) and I matched up against Danny and Pete Gray in a duel that reached the final stages before Walker once again delved into his bag of tricks. It happened like this:

I was about to attempt a three-foot putt to give my side the win when Danny suddenly collapsed onto the green, arms and legs spread , and lay just to the front and right of my line of vision. Anyone else's swoon would have stopped play and started medical assistance. But his friends knew Danny too well and always expected the unexpected from him. Thus, we ignored him as he lay motionless on his back, arms and legs spread, looking all the world as if he were dead. With Danny just a couple of feet from my putter, I sank the putt and Charlie and I collected our winnings.

I have not seen Danny in many years. He doesn't stay in one place for very long. Last I heard, he was somewhere in the Dallas area running some obscure business with his second wife, an LSUS graduate. She, I heard, was smart enough to appoint herself the company treasurer and bookkeeper. Otherwise, the Walker earnings would probably end up in some sandbagger's pockets on the 19th hole.

Cat Tales

Although I prefer dogs to cats, I feel that I owe cats some ink space because a number of my writings have been about dogs while none have been about cats.

So this is about two cats that I have reluctantly "owned."

In the 1980s, a couple of teenagers bestowed upon my children, Jonathan and Leigh-Ann, a black and white feline by the cognomen of Moon-Unit. Mooner, as Leigh-Ann preferred to call her, was named, I believe, for Moon-Unit Zappa.

Moon-Unit Tabor was very much on the moody side. She spent most of her time lying around ignoring me and expecting humans to take care of all her basic needs such as feeding, watering, grooming, and freshening the litter box. In other words, Mooner was a normal cat.

As for her emotional needs, she usually couldn't care less about receiving affection unless it was her idea to get close, and given during a time of her choosing. After a day of getting along perfectly without my attention, Mooner, late at night, changed from Miss Iceberg, to Miss Warmth. Precisely at 10:30 p.m. when I started to get comfortable with Johnny and *The Tonight Show*, Mooner would hop onto the sofa and stalk over to my lap, where she curled up and purred and rubbed her head against my belly without asking for permission. No longer aloof and distant, she demanded strokes and plenty of them. The next day she would return to her other self, cool and remote.

Mooner did not like dogs. When a friendly one came playfully into the open garage one day, Mooner reared back on two legs and went into an attack mode with sharp, flailing claws aimed at the intruder's face. The bleeding dog, four or five times the size of Mooner, never retaliated. But he kept his distance.

There is additional evidence of Mooner's distrust of dogs. One night I was driving home to southeast Shreveport with Mooner on board. Because my friend Conway lived nearby, I thought I would pop in and introduce him to Mooner. I didn't worry about anything going wrong because I knew that

Conway kept his German shorthaired pointer, W.F. Woodfreckle, in his fenced-in backyard. What I didn't know was that Conway's daughter, Anne, was visiting. Also visiting was her dog Sting.

With Mooner under my arm, I rang the doorbell. When the door opened, I was greeted not only by Conway but also Sting. As soon as Mooner saw Sting, she became a climber, and my chest and face became Everest. It is difficult to describe the unexpected pain of a series of cat claws going up your face. Just believe that the agony level rates quite high when you consider that her claws in my cheeks provided excellent traction for her ascent.

Mooner moved rapidly up my face; however, once she reached the summit, namely the top of my head, she dug into my scalp something fierce.

How does one remove a panic-stricken cat from one's head? With much difficulty. The more I tugged at Mooner, the deeper she dug in. I thought I might have to drive home with a cat on my head and wondered if doing that would be in violation of Shreveport traffic laws.

Finally, with Sting out of sight, Mooner relaxed her grip, and I extracted her along with half of my hair.

Ever wonder about the origin of the words *catastrophe* and *catastrophic*? They were invented by people who had cats.

Moving on...

The cat that is the focus of the second half of this article was known only as Roykin, not Roykin Tabor. The reason for this surname omission centers around the fact that Roykin didn't really **belong** to anyone. He was his own cat. He could not be owned.

Nevertheless, long after Mooner disappeared for good, Roykin, in the early nineties, sorta adopted me as his sometime guardian.

Roykin was named after the owner and builder of my old house on Bruce Avenue in Shreveport, Roy Herring. Mr. Herring, had died in the house and somehow it was felt that this new cat, who mysteriously showed up one day, was kin to Roy in spirit, if not the spirit of Roy himself.

When Roykin first started hanging around, sympathetic me began to supply him with water and vittles. Most of the time Roykin appeared to appreciate my efforts. Other times, he seemed possessed by an evil spirit unlike that of his namesake. For example, when I lounged in walk shorts in the backyard, sometimes Roykin would saunter by and suddenly give my legs a good clawing. An unprovoked clawing. Roykin for sure needed a cat shrink.

Rokykin invented the expression "tom-catting around." He often stayed away for a week at a time, then would stagger home, de-furred, tired, and hungry. After he got his water and provisions, he would then sleep for two or three days. Then after being a homebody for a week, off he would go, and the pattern would repeat itself.

Sometimes Roykin's wild nightlife would be experienced at home. Often I was awakened at night by the sounds of cat fighting. The next morning the evidence was clearly seen: cat fur littered the back yard.

Roykin's activities soon came to a sad end. One day he seemed overly listless, with absolutely no appetite. Day after day he went downhill so rapidly that employing a veterinarian would have been useless. Roykin was dying from ingesting something like anti-freeze. I made him as comfortable as possible in a straw-filled box with a little water beside him and waited for the end.

Although I have "owned" just these two cats, I do not pretend to understand them as I understand dogs. My friend Jack Nolan, the New York state transplant, has half dozen cats that apparently left an impression the last time I was in the Nolan house because the other night I dreamed his cats were prancing about like kings and queens, ruling the Nolan household with Jack and his wife Chris as their subjects. The cats took whatever they wanted, including all the Friskies they desired. They suffocated Jack and Chris with their moodiness and went from room to room carving out choice, comfortable cat spots. The human being Nolans did all the giving, the cat Nolans all the receiving.

I awoke in cold perspiration and struggled throughout the day to rid this nightmare from my consciousness, knowing this dream could actually become a reality if the Nolan cats, Nemo, Mick, Thelma, Coco, and Willie, were to get their clawed paws on a copy of David Greene's 207-page book, *Your Incredible Cat,* subtitled *Understanding the Secret Powers of Your Pet.*

Greene's book promises to take readers deep inside the secret and mysterious world of cats, exploring the extraordinary mental and psychic skills and powers that cats possess. *Your Incredible Cat* includes stories of cats that exhibit amazing intelligence and ability to communicate, even clairvoyance and mind control. Yes, in my imagination I see a stupefied Jack Nolan saying to Chris in a flat, inflectionless, mesmeric voice: "Must… buy…catnip. Must…buy…catnip. Must ..buy…'

The Perils of Plagiarism

During my career in academia I made it a point each semester to spend a few minutes discussing with my students the subject of plagiarism.

In addition to emphasizing the dishonesty and immorality of lifting another writer's work and claiming it as their own, I made sure the students understood that plagiarism penalties would be severe, perhaps expulsion from the class and/or the university itself.

During the plagiarism pep talk one could hear the proverbial pin drop. A very quiet classroom. Grave facial expressions. Had some already committed the sin of plagiarism, perhaps in their hearts?

In a thirty-seven year career in education, thirty-three at LSU in Shreveport, I discovered three cases of students copying the writing of another author. The first two were in the early years: one just before 1970, the other some time into the '70s. The first and last were at LSUS; the second occurred on the campus of Wiley College in Marshall, Texas, where I did some part-time teaching briefly in the 70s.

Let's take the cases in chronological order.

Shortly after I began at LSUS in 1968, the university's second year of existence, I encountered the first act of plagiarism. A student in a freshman composition class turned in a paper that seemed extremely familiar. It was familiar because I had originally read the article a couple of weeks earlier in *The* (Shreveport) *Times*. Not only was this student being foolishly risky with his academic career, he was not making good use of his God–given brain cells. Why should he assume that I did not read *The Times*? As I think about it, maybe he believed it was more professorial to read only the *Times* of New York or the *Times* of London. Or even *The Los Angeles Times*. But I doubt it.

The second case took place at Wiley, where once again in a composition class, the plagiarism alarm went off shortly after I began reading a student essay. It seems the student had copied word for word from a textbook that

I used at LSUS. He, of course, gambled that I would not be familiar with the text, nor the particular essay that he lifted. He gambled and lost, and suffered as a result.

The third case occurred in the 1990s at LSUS. The crime was committed by a journalism student who was close to graduation. I liked this student and sympathized with her domestic situation as a single, working mother whose own mother suffered from lupus.

I suppose this student could not imagine that I would subscribe to a number of obscure health magazines. From one of those publications, she copied, verbatim, an article about eggs and their impact on people's health. The only thing she changed was the title. Before I had finished reading her lead paragraph, the plagiarism alarm went off.

Because this case is the most recent, I am able to remember more details, especially those of the moment that I had to inform her of her criminality.

My desire was to teach, not to humiliate. Therefore, at the end of class I asked her to meet me back in the classroom later that afternoon. At the appointed time, I went to the classroom, somewhat darkened with only the light from the windows providing illumination, with her feature story in one hand and the magazine in the other.

I felt awkward and sad and embarrassed for her. And I had no idea what to say. So, I simply placed on the desk at which she was sitting, the magazine, turned open to the copied article. Next to it, I put her typed paper.

The ensuing silence was long and deafening. Neither of us spoke. Finally, her eyes began to tear. I don't remember our words when we eventually broke the stillness, but neither of us enjoyed that scene.

These three students took a chance and were caught cheating. I am sure that through the years many others cheated without being discovered. We who attempt to guide and train students cannot be aware of every published word, each printed sentence, and the myriad written paragraphs.

Unfortunately, this problem is not helped at all by those on the internet who offer students for a sum of money, various essays that utilize rhetorical devices such as exemplification, narration, causal analysis, comparison and contrast, etc. Students most likely are easily tempted by their advertisements.

Sadly, the act of plagiarism represents the unfortunate choices of too many of today's citizens, whose focus seems to be on the quick, easy way, the way of little work. Somewhere during the evolution of this country too many folks have convinced themselves that what is important is achieving the goal by any means with little thought given to how that goal is achieved.

Dark-Alley Choices

Someone once asked me, "If you were walking through the darkest, scariest alley in America and you could choose only one person to accompany you, who would it be?"

You mean someone like Arnold Schwarzenegger?

"No. A real person. Someone you actually know. Someone from Homer. Someone from Claiborne Parish."

I thought of close relatives: cousins, uncles, and even father. Where there is a skirmish, blood runs thicker than water. Especially if you are in the right on the issue.

As I mulled through the names of various relatives, an old episode from *Bonanza* came to mind: Facing one of their many crises, the Cartwright sons gathered around their father, Ben, to discuss their dilemma. Ben squatted near the Ponderosa ground, picked up a twig, paused for dramatic effect, then snapped the twig into.

"This is what happens when we go it alone," he said. Then Ben grabbed up a HANDFUL of sticks: an old graying one, a short one, a middle-size stick, and a hearty, fat stick. He attempted to break the bunch without success. You could see the lights go on for Hoss: "Dadgum. If we stick together, they can't break us." Adam looked smug and rolled his eyes. Little Joe smirked and his eyes twinkled with excessive confidence. Adam and Little Joe turned to Hoss and said, "Duhhh."

As I continued mulling through my list of relatives as a choice, I did not rule out my dad, C.L. Tabor, Jr., 87. He was considered as a nominee because of a story I heard about him a couple of years ago. The story tellers were my Aunt Gladys and Uncle Tommy, who live in Minden. They told me that a few short years before the story-telling, they took a little vacation trip with Mom and Dad. During the journey they stopped at a restaurant for a bite to eat. They were enjoying themselves to the max when from the next booth came the sounds of four-letter words from a group of four men.

I suppose Mom and Gladys and Tommy were too involved in their own conversation to notice too much. Not Dad. As the loud cussing continued, Dad grew quieter and quieter. The foul language went on. Suddenly Dad was out of his seat and on his feet. He whipped out his little pocketknife, opened the blade, and held it toward the guys with the trashy mouths.

"There are LADIES here!" he said emphatically. "I want that kind of language to stop!"

It did. Dad returned to his seat. No more cuss words were heard. Right makes might.

But the idea of picking family to take that walk through the alley became academic when my mind–reading friend who dreamed up this game narrowed the field further: "No relatives," he said. So it was back to the drawing board.

"Well, Tabor, who would you pick?"

I mulled over the hypothetical setting and thought aloud: "darkest, scariest alley in America…one person…Claiborne Parish…

"That would be either Peanut Covington or Dooley Peterson," I said. And of course my questioner wanted to know why.

Julius "Dooley" Peterson I don't know as well as Charles "Peanut" Covington. My earliest memory of Dooley was when I was a little kid and he was a big kid who sometimes ran around with my neighbor Marion Henry White.

Later, in the mid nineties I became a relatively distant neighbor of his on Lake Claiborne. Sometimes our paths would cross when we walked our dogs: my black labs and his Shar Pei, a no-nonsense dog who barked at me for four years every time I walked past the Peterson house. But I like dogs who protect their turf, and I admire their owners who do the same.

The conclusion that Dooley is a no-nonsense guy is based a lot on the writings of Dr. T.M. Deas, who has often told about Dooley in his *Guardian-Journal* column, "Olden Times." Dr. Deas' classic and unforgettable story about Dooley recounts the time when a crowd of jeering, scoffing Neville High School supporters taunted a busload of Homerites after Neville's 20-0 playoff win over the Pelicans. Like my dad, I suppose Dooley reach his limit of what he could take. As Dr. Deas tells the story, Dooley came out of the bus "fighting mad," ready to take on the entire town of Monroe.

Right makes might.

Charles "Peanut" Covington, on the other hand, I have known for a long time and in close fashion. Peanut is a really nice guy, was Mr. Pelican at Homer High School, has a wonderful sense of humor, and loves Burt Lancaster movies. There are many heroic Peanut Covington stories, but the one that best exemplifies his being a no-nonsense guy took place when he and I were students at Louisiana Tech. One night Peanut, Joe Simpson, John David Brantly, Butch Fincher, and I went over to Ruston High School to see a football game between the Bearcats and Winnfield.

Sometime during the game, perhaps at the half, as the four of us were standing near the bleachers, we were approached by four or five scowling young men that we had never seen. The one scowling the most poked a finger at Joe's nose and accused him and his buddies of insulting his girlfriend. And we were going to pay for it.

My immediate thought was that these guys had taken us for someone else. John David, Joe, and Butch must have been trying to decode the surprising accusations as well.

Peanut didn't buy it for a second. He was handing his watch and class ring to the rest of us and rolling up his sleeves to do battle. When Peanut was finished with the sleeves, the smallest member of our adversaries, as if on cue, tugged at the ringleader's arm and said, "Hey, Skipper, these ain't the guys. These ain't the guys. Let's go."

Skipper turned his head. "You say these ain't the guys, Booger? These ain't the guys?"

"No, Skipper. These AIN'T the guys."

Our new friends began to back away, mumbling something about a mistaken identity. But Peanut didn't buy it. He didn't buy their nonsense for a second. He called their bluff before the rest of us could make any sense of what was happening.

When we shared this story with a Tech student from Winnfield, he laughed. "Yeah, I know those guys. They're little creeps always looking for trouble. They're nothing."

Right makes might.

So, my dark alley non-relative, Claiborne Parish choices would be Charles "Peanut" Covington or Julius "Dooley" Peterson. And if my friend who dreamed up this hypothetical would stretch his rules a little, I would have one of these guys on each side as together, we went down that scary, dark alley. I, of course, would be in the middle with my pen and pad, taking names.

A Rebel With Tiger Stripes

The size Small purple Team Starter football jersey hangs docile-like in my clothes closet, feeling somewhat misplaced and overwhelmed by an array of Extra Large dress shirts, polo shirts, pullovers. It hangs patiently, waiting for the appropriate day in late December when it journeys from Louisiana to Mississippi from gray-haired grandfather to tow-headed grandson.

The future recipient is Andrew Bailey Tabor, who will, in the time to come, find himself perhaps an unwilling participant in the ancient and exciting Southeastern Conference football rivalry between Louisiana State University and the University of Mississippi. Poor Bailey. Only three years old, he is destined to become something of a Rebel with Tiger stripes.

That's because his Mississippi grandfather, Duane Gosa, is a die-hard Ole Miss football fan. Otherwise, Grandpa Gosa seems a decent fellow. He and I are poised to lock ourselves into perpetual mortal combat over Bailey's soul and SEC allegiance.

It is possible that I have struck first against the enemy, with the mesh jersey that sports a white number 14 trimmed in gold, front and back. To make sure that Bailey understands the gift's significance, on the jersey back, above the number are the white letters LSU, also trimmed in gold, along with the head of a growling tiger the size of a half dollar on the front shoulder.

Unfortunately, PapPaw Gosa has home field advantage, living just across town from Bailey, in Jackson. To offset this "time of possession" edge, I am prepared to adjust my bedtime story–telling repertoire by replacing *Jack and the Beanstalk* with the wondrous tale of *Billy and the Halloween Run*.

As soon as he is capable of understanding, Bailey will know that Billy Cannon's ephemeral 89-yard punt return against the No. 2-nationally ranked Ole Miss Rebels on October 31, 1959, catapulted the No. 1 Tigers to a 7-3 victory in a match-up that has been voted the "game of the decade" by the Southeastern Conference.

And when it's still and quiet I can sometimes hear the radio announcer's bygone cry rising in a frenzied crescendo: "Billy Cannon watches it bounce. He takes it on his own eleven. He comes back up the field to the fifteen, stumbles momentarily; he's at the twenty, running hard at the twenty-five. Gets away from one man at the thirty, still running at the twenty-five…at the thirty-five…at the forty-five. He's going to the fifty. He's in the kicker… forty-five, forty, thirty-five, thirty, twenty-five, twenty, fifteen, ten , five. He scores!"

As an immediate result of the run, multitudes became Tiger fans, and the legend can easily hatch new converts if it is told just right. Bailey may also find intriguing the fact that a Haynesville resident (some say demented) was so moved by the run that he re-named himself Billy Cannon.

That's really carrying things a bit too far. Much too far.

At the same time, notice how the name Bailey Cannon Tabor rolls off the tongue with such ease.

Letter to Bailey

Dear Bailey,

You can stop asking your mother if you're four yet. You, Andrew Bailey Tabor, my only grandson, the infamous Rebel in Tiger Stripes, are four years old today.

At your birthday party at Chick–Fil–A tomorrow perhaps some of your presents will be more Dr. Seuss books. I know how much you enjoy those that line your bookcase in your bedroom. One of them is really special. It is called *Hop on Pop*. When your dad was four and your Aunt Leigh was two, this was their favorite book. They especially enjoyed it whenever I lay in bed with them and read it aloud. Whenever I reached the page where the little bears hopped on their pop, your dad and Aunt Leigh began to hop on their pop: me, Pepaw. Sometimes I tried to skip those pages, but they were too smart for me. They turned the pages back and hopped on their pop. Now I want you to carry on this way of having fun. Get your dad to read you *Hop on Pop* and when he reaches the "hop-on" page, get your little sister Riley to help you hop on your pop. You will love it!

Remember when your dad took you to a real movie theater to see *Finding Nemo*? I heard that you liked it so much that you sat quietly through the whole show. When I was your age, one of the best movies of all time was made. It is called *Casablanca* and some day when you are older, you will want to see it. It was not in color like *Nemo*. Back then, in the 1940s, not many movies were made in color like they are today. It was made in black and white, but don't let that keep you from seeing it. Your dad really liked his first black and white movie, which he saw when he was eleven years old. It was called *The Elephant Man*, a sad but good story about a man who suffered from a terrible, deforming disease. This is a movie that you need to be a little older to see, maybe eleven like your dad was.

Remember when your cousin Anna Banana had her tonsils out last spring? I was about your age when my tonsils were taken out. It was in a place called Highland Hospital in a city in Louisiana called Shreveport, about the size of the city where you live, Jackson. The best thing I remember about being in the hospital was getting color crayons and a coloring book.

When I was the same age as you, the country we live in, the United States of America, was a member of a group of countries called the Allies. The Allies were fighting some other countries to keep themselves free. These other countries joined together and called themselves the Axis. Some of those small airplanes in your bedroom are called Grumman F4F Wildcats. Our country used real planes like these and soldiers to fly them to win that war. Even though our country won, it still fights wars today. The first big war like this was supposed to be the war to end all wars. You are smart enough to understand that it did not. My prayer is that by the time you grow up and become a man like your daddy, there will be no more wars.

During the last part of this terrible war your great grandpa, C.L. Tabor Jr., was a United States soldier stationed overseas in another country. I was just about the age you are now when I sent letters to him. These letters were a lot like those you may have seen on Mommy and Daddy's computer screen, except that they were on paper. This is the way people used to write letters to each other. Because I really could not write at that time, I told my mother, your great grandma, what to say for me and she wrote the words exactly as I said them. With one of the letters I also drew him a picture of a house with two windows and a door and front steps and two people with funny looking hair and no feet. Great Grandpa and Great Grandma saved this drawing for fifty-eight years. I will bring the picture for you to see when I come to your birthday party on Friday.

Bailey, I am going to share parts of one letter that I sent to your great grandfather from a small town called Arcadia. I sent it to him on August 4, 1945.

Dear Daddy,
I sure do wish I could see you.
    What are you going to bring me when you come home?
    Why don't you send my rations to me?
    I will draw you some more things.
    Is it hot over there?

When I had my tonsils taken out I got lots of pretties (toys). Have you forgotten about me having my tonsils taken out?

There are lots of troop trains that come by here.

I wish you could come see my pretties.

When you come home, are you going to give me a present?

Send me some letters, too. You send Mama letters and don't send me any. When you send me lots of letters, send Mama lots of letters.

I love you lots,
Love,
Randall

Bailey, ask your mom or dad to read this to you. I will send you more letters as you learn to read. Learning to read is very important. If you can read, you can do anything you want to do and be anything you want to be. If you learn to read, maybe you can even help the world to stop having wars.

Bailey, through the past four years I have watched you grow into a fine young man. You are truly a gift from God. Being your grandfather makes me very happy. I love you.

Pepaw

Letter to Pepaw

Madison, Mississippi
March 6, 2009

Dear Pepaw,
How are you? I am still thinking about you and all of ya'll in my head.
I think LSU is going to be UP UP and amazing. Before you know it
we will be #1. You are awesome. I love you!!! I got contacts. They feel
funny!!! I think Frazier (dog) misses you too! I am starting baseball
so you can come. Oh, and at the bottom there is a warning.

Love
Yours,
Bailey

warning
write back

Love Those Jerbs

As I was putting the finishing touches on my state income tax return, following the IRS last month putting the finishing touch on me, I wondered how I could recoup my own money lost to the government.

The answer is jerbs.

Living in the mecca of capitalism, I wanted to come up with an income-producing idea that Americans would be willing to buy and something that would require from me as little time and overhead as possible.

I thought about those marvelously successful products of the seventies, like mood rings and Pet Rocks. The inventor of the Pet Rock, Gary Dahl, marketed his product so well that more than a million people bought Rocks as Christmas gifts in 1975. In a few weeks' time, Dahl was a millionaire, and Rocks were America's No. 1 pet, surpassing the more responsive Labrador retriever.

If it worked for Dahl in 1975, maybe it could work for Tabor in 2011. Hopefully, thirty-six years is enough time for Americans to forget how stupid they can be.

So I took a break from taxes and thought. The product had to be something that demanded of me little money, little time, and little work. The best thing I could come up with was nothing. That's right, selling my fellow Americans nothing. I could see the exciting potential of selling nothing. Nothing takes up no space, requires no food or water, and nothing does not have to be cleaned. The only thing I needed at this point was a name for nothing. American consumers may be stupid, but they are not about to buy nothing without a name.

For a name, I could simply pick letters at random and come up with something like *blonzkeft*. But then I remembered a word that Dad sometimes used as a noun to describe certain persons. I thought perhaps he brought the word *jerb* home from World War II, like the word *Kilroy*.

I was a fully grown man before I got around to asking Dad about *jerb*. One day in the TV room of his home I said to him, "Dad, what is a jerb?"

He didn't know. Hey, he only *used* the word. "I first heard your Uncle Elton use *jerb* ," he explained. "I don't know where he got it." Uncle Elton was deceased, so I couldn't ask him.

So, since *jerb* is a word with no known definition, it seemed to be the perfect name to market my nothing product. Now with a name, jerbs could command consumer respect. Jerbs could easily fit inside gift bags and boxes of varying sizes, depending on how big a jerb you wanted and how much you wanted to spend.

If jerbs could meet the success of the Pet Rock, then I could picture at Christmastime a battered but proud soccer mom returning home from the local Mallmart, saying in exhausted tones to her six-year-old, "Susie, precious, Mommie fought through hundreds of other mommies to get you the very last Jerb in the store. That's how much Mommie loves you!"

Little Susie would reply, "Gee, Mom, now that I have a Jerb, I will also be loved by all my classmates. You're such a swell mom. But, hey, watch it! The blood from your nose is dripping onto my Jerb!"

On a cautionary note we entrepreneurs must be prepared for the worst. What if there is a recession? Or a depression? What if consumers don't want nothing for $9.99? Just in case Americans are smarter than they were in 1975, despite the lack of tangible evidence, then maybe I could at least have a little fun using *jerb* as a word.

Before I retired, I used to challenge my students at LSU in Shreveport to do a little lexicographic experiment. I contended that each and every one them in the classroom had the ability to add to the vocabulary of accepted English words. All they had to do to succeed with the test was to go about the campus, their various classrooms, student government meetings, Greek get-togethers, etc, and, at these places, in the midst of others, drop into their conversations a word of their invention. I advised them to simply pick consonants and vowels at random, like *delsot*. They were urged to use their creation as any or many parts of speech: noun, verb, modifier, whatever. Like, for example: "Jennifer, you're such a jerb!"

Or: "Shameeka, you're disjerbing me, and don't like it!"

Or: "Man, that tractor-pull last Sunday was totally jerbsome!"

I advised the students to use the word often and inconspicuously, but to also be careful not to overdo its use. If they heeded the advice, I predicted, they could expect other students to begin to use *delsot* or *sodlet* or whatever they came up with. The use of this invented word would spread throughout Shreveport into the Ark-La-Tex and eventually to all parts of the world. I told the students that they should celebrate their creation as soon as Dan Rather said, "Vice-president Dan Quayle today put his jerb in his mouth."

Disavowing the adage, "Those who can, do; those who can't, teach," I will take my professorial advice and do."

Imagine the possible scenarios:

A staunch Republican might say to his Democrat friend: "Only a jerb would have voted for Barrack Obama."

Or telephone companies, in their continued greedy quest for money and confused customers, could add mysterious jerb charges to phone bills.

Doctors who don't know what the heck is ailing their patients could use *jerb:* "Mrs. Landrum, you have a jerb. Take aspirin, drink plenty of fluids, and get lots of rest."

Or for those insufferable hypochondriacs who are not happy unless they are sick, doctors could say: "Mrs. Staudinger, you can brag to the members of your sewing circle that you officially have a case of jerbitus. Thank God we caught it in time. Take these (placebo) pills and call me in three years."

Unemployed losers like George Costanza could try to impress women by saying to them, "I export jerbs." The bimbos, not wanting to appear stupid, would reply, "Oh, that's nice." I fathomed the psychology behind this technique a few years ago when my friend Conway and I went to an evening estate sale in Shreveport. There were items galore, but one in particular caught my eye. I had absolutely no idea what the device was. I picked it up and wondered what in the world it could possibly be used for. As I turned the metal apparatus this way and that way in my hands, a stranger moved next to me.

"What is that?" he asked.

Being in a playful mood I immediately answered, "It's a reekle bucket."

The man, not wanting to seem ignorant, cupped his chin and pretended to think. "Oh, indeed it is. Of course."

Conway, overhearing the dialogue, jumped right in. "John!" he exclaimed. "A reekle bucket! It's been years since I've seen one!"

For the rest of the evening the stranger seemed to follow us from room to room with a look of awe. Not surprising, since Conway and I were omniscient gods.

Jerb in a Jar, Serious Inquiries Only

Because of Jerbs' lack of mass and volume, they would likely fit inside gift bags and boxes of almost any size. *Jars* might also serve as Jerb containers, especially if it's a really old Jerb you're selling.

My Jerb idea was somewhat validated when someone offered for sale on e-Bay a ghost in a jar. According to the seller, back in the early eighties, while out metal detecting, he came across an old abandoned cemetery with the foundation of a home site or church or some type of building nearby.

When this guy's detector indicated something in the southwest vicinity of the foundation, he dug two feet to find a somewhat rotted wooden box. In the box, he says, were a journal and two jars decorated with strange writing and symbols. While getting the jars out of the ground, he dropped one. It broke and apparently released the pent-up ghost inside. The ghost manifested itself as a black mist.

Leaving the broken jar, he took home the other jar and the journal. He writes: "What I was able to read in the journal before the pages crumbled made the hair on the back of my neck stand up." The seller doesn't say on the e-Bay web site what exactly raised his neck hair. Apparently you receive that information when you purchase the ghost in a jar.

The seller continues: "That night I had my first visit from what I can only describe as 'The Black Thing.' While lying in bed, this 'thing' fell on me and it felt like I was being pushed down thru the bed and the floor, into a pit if you will! I struggled with it and managed to somehow escape its clutches."

Since that time, he says, he has been attacked twice more by the black, shadowy thing. Both times the unopened jar was in close vicinity.

Finally speaking with someone who is "versed in these things," he was told that the only way to rid himself of the ghost was to pass the unopened jar on to someone else. Therefore, he is offering it to you and me and the general public, via e-Bay.

He established a beginning bid price of $99 for the ghost in a jar, somewhat high considering that I plan to sell Jerbs for the quite affordable $9.99. His explanation for setting the high reserve: to insure that someone SERIOUS can own the ghost. "Yes, I COULD give it away or sell it for a buck or two…" but somehow he feels that it should be SOLD to the appropriate person "with a knowledge of these things."(or with an ownership of cash)

The seller warns that once you buy the ghost in a jar, it is yours, and that he will have nothing ever again to do with it. All sales are final, of course. The seller refuses to ship the ghost in the jar through the post office. The buyer's choices are to go with UPS or to pay the seller to deliver the ghost himself. You must contact the seller within twenty-four hours of the close of the sale to make payment arrangements.

And there's this caveat in huge capital letters: "I WILL NOT BE HELD RESPONSIBLE FOR ANYTHING THAT HAPPENS ONCE THE TRANSACTION IS COMPLETE!" (like maybe the ghost never actually making an appearance) If the ghost *does* happen to appear and you feel you've gotten more than you really wanted, re-burying the jar does no good. The seller tried that with no end to the visits from the ghost.

Apparently some surfers are starting to play with this guy. A copycat ghost in a jar has emerged. But the original ghost owner has the audacity to warn us that the owner of the ghost-come-lately is trying to con us. He writes, "Mimicry may be the highest form of flattery but they are riduculous." (sic)

And despite a violation of e-Bay rules and maybe even federal trade laws, astronomical bids have been pouring in. To date, the highest bid is $999,999,999 for the original ghost in a jar.

But why pay that much for a ghost of mischief and mayhem when you can get a loving and docile Jerb for $999,999,989.01 less? Just send me your credit card number and the expiration date and I'll promptly ship your very own Jerb in a Jar. Postage and handling included in the purchase price. But only if you're someone serious.

A Few of My Favorite Things

Although I have never made a list of New Year' resolutions, I consider myself as a list guy. I find interesting people's choices for the best, the worst, the weirdest, the funniest of just about anything. The following are my favorite various and sundry things past and present:

Non-living novelist, W. Somerset Maugham

Work by non-living novelist, *The Razor's Edge*

Runner-up non-living novelist, William Styron

Work by runner-up novelist, *Sophie's Choice*

Short story, "The Eighty-Yard Run," by Irwin Shaw

Black and white film, *Casablanca*

Color film, (tie) *The Godfather* and *The Godfather II*

Actress, Meryl Streep

Actor, Robert DeNiro

Single performance by an actor, Ed Harris in *Pollock*

Single performance by an actress, Natalie Wood in *Splendor in the Grass*

Dancer, Fred Astaire

Movie song, *As Time Goes By* (Casablanca)

Horror film, *The Sixth Sense*

Scary film, *Phantasm*

"A-western film, *The Wild Bunch*

"A"-western performance, Gary Cooper in *High Noon*

"B"-western film star (singer division) Roy Rogers

"B"-western film star (non–singer division) The Durango Kid (Charles Starrett)

"B"-western backup singers, Sons of the Pioneers

"B"-western sidekick, Gabby Hayes

"B"-western horse, Trigger (smartest horse in the movies)

Comic strip, *Beetle Bailey*

Comic book, *BOY Comics*

Immortal superhero (homo sapiens division), Superman

Immortal superhero (rodent division) Mighty Mouse

Mortal superhero, Batman

Professional basketball player, Bob Petit

Professional football player, Frank Gifford

Quarterback, Joe Montana

Position baseball player, Joe DiMaggio

Pitcher, Sandy Koufax

Golfer, Arnold Palmer

Sitcom, *Seinfeld*

Comic duo, Bob and Ray

Family TV show, *Andy Griffith*

TV sci-fi, (tie) the original *Outer Limits* and *Star Trek*

Sci-fi movie, *The Andromeda Strain*

Scariest book, *The Exorcist*

Romantic movie, *Marjorie Morningstar*

Comedy, *Planes, Trains, and Automobiles*

Rock and Roll performer, Elvis Presley

Rock and Roll song, *Don't Be Cruel* by Elvis Presley

Country and western performer, Hank Williams

Country and western song, *Kaw-liga* by Hank Williams

Rock and Roll group, The Eagles

Late-night talk show host, Johnny Carson

Weird stand-up comic, Jonathan Winters

Funny stand-up comic, George Carlin

Sportscaster, Bob Costas

Dramatic TV show, *Playhouse 90*

TV western, *The Virginian*

TV Adventure, *Adventures in Paradise* (starring Gardner McKay)

Fifteen-minute TV Show, *Coke Time* (with Eddie Fisher)

Cartoon character, Mickey Mouse

Cartoon duo, Heckle and Jeckle

Non-cheese pizza ingredient, green peppers

Commercial ice cream, Blue Bell

Soft drink, Coca-Cola

Commercially fried chicken, Popeye's

Commercially fried onion rings, Popeye's

Snack food, peanut butter

Candy bar, Butterfinger

Sugar substitute, stevia

Car for the money, Lexus

Marketing mistake, the old new Coke without fizz

High school class, mechanical drawing

College class, European history

Toy, Slinky

Day of the week, Friday

Season, spring

Month, May

Scam, Jerbs

The Joe Michael College
Clothing Allowance

In August of 1962 I graduated from Louisiana Tech with a B.A. degree in English education and a minor in journalism. In an earlier column I thanked my parents, C.L. and Gracie Tabor, for their sacrifices in footing 99.99 percent of the cost of my undergraduate education but never thanked the person responsible for my college clothing allowance.

Back in the fifties and sixties college students wore coats, ties, and hats to events like football games just as an earlier generation decked out in suits to attend informal affairs such as movies and baseball games.

From 1958–1962 and for a period beyond 1962 Joe Michael, proprietor of Michael's Men's Store, was my primary clothier, for a number of reasons: (1) great clothing, (2) great service, and (3) outstanding terms. Want outstanding terms? Try an unspecified line of credit at zero percent interest. Without Joe Michael's generous terms I would have been sorely underdressed when Stan Kenton and his orchestra serenaded dancing Tech students in the basketball gymnasium and when the Bulldogs battled Northwestern at State Fair Stadium in Shreveport.

Usually whenever I got home from Ruston on weekends, I'd make a beeline to Michael's Men's Store. "Is my credit still good?" I'd ask.

"SURE, your credit's good," Joe Michael would reply without hesitation. Then he'd start pulling out Van Heusen shirts, Prince Consort ties, Botany 500 suits, Nunn Bush shoes, socks , and belts.

But he really wasn't in the suit-selling business as much as the suit-FITTING business. Wouldn't let me out of the store if he wasn't pleased with the fit. Wanted me to look *good*. So, as much as heaven would allow, Joe Michael made me look good. And when his customers looked good, he was happy.

Aided by summer job paychecks from the Homer Tobacco, Candy & Drug Company I chipped away at the balance due Michael's Men's Store and finally paid my debt. But when I moved to south Louisiana in the mid sixties, my visits to Michael's Men's Store became seldom if ever. Then in August of 1968, fresh out of graduate school I began a thirty-three year career at LSU in Shreveport, where in 1968, faculty members were in the habit of wearing coats and ties. Therefore, I went home to Homer and Michael's Men's Store to get properly outfitted.

"Is my credit still good?" I asked Joe Michael.

"SURE, your credit's good," he said without hesitation. Weeks later I was back in Homer with a friend and colleague, Jim Miller, professor of history. Seems Jim was so impressed with my new attire that he insisted that I show him the way to Michael's Men's Store. As I recall, Joe Michael also extended credit to the Cajun from Crowley, La. A complete stranger to him.

That's the story of how Joe Michael indirectly helped to finance my college education by selling me clothing on credit. He took a gamble on a kid with no job security and never sent a bill.

Thoughts of EWE

From nowhere the other day thoughts of former Louisiana governor Edwin W. Edwards came to mind. Edwin must be getting really tired of prison life at the Federal Correctional Institution in Oakdale, Louisiana.

Why did he suddenly burst into my brain? Could it be that he's telepathically sending messages for me to begin a "Free Edwards" campaign for his early release? Probably not. He's lasted almost ten years behind bars and is finally scheduled for release in July of 2011. Besides, such campaigns have been attempted before, to no avail. Most notably, former Louisiana Republican governor David Treen unsuccessfully went to bat for Edwards, a populist Democrat. For three years Treen petitioned Presidents George W. Bush and George H.W. Bush to commute Edwards' sentence. "Even if Governor Edwards were guilty of what he was convicted, he certainly never stole a dime from taxpayers," Treen said.

In 2000 Edwards was convicted on seventeen of twenty-six federal counts, including racketeering, extortion, money laundering, mail fraud and wire fraud.

The first time I met Edwards was at the beginning of the seventies when he was in his early forties on the newborn LSU in Shreveport campus, where I was the PR guy. Edwards had come from Crowley to kick start his first gubernatorial campaign to replace John McKeithen in 1972. As soon as he stepped from his car, I was there to greet him and shake hands. His were a bit moist. Was the charming, confident Edwin Edwards not as confident as his persona? Perhaps not that day. In time the level of assurance would undoubtedly climb into the stratosphere where it was obviously located when he later said, prior to an election: "I could not lose unless I was caught in bed with a dead girl or a live boy."

Years after our initial meeting, amidst one of his four governorships, we shook paws again, in the Petroleum Tower in downtown Shreveport, This time his hand was as dry as a Palm Springs talc shop. Interesting what a little political success can do for the psyche.

Anyway, his confidence must have gotten a major boost back on that day in the seventies at LSU in Shreveport where the secretaries and coeds swooned in his pathway as I escorted him through the school's three meager buildings. (LSUS opened in September of 1967.) There was a chorus of drawn-out exclamations like, "Oh, he's so handsome." Especially when he pecked them on the cheek. I suppose, for women, handsomeness probably registers near the top of the political criteria list along with lesser issues like taxes and welfare.

After Edwards became governor he returned to LSUS and spoke in the tiny Science Lecture Auditorium, reputed to have the least-comfortable seats of any assembly room in existence. Nevertheless, the place was packed with students, faculty, administrators, and the politically curious from off campus. In fact, it was standing room only.

No politician has ever given a speech without at least one promise. EWE was no exception. "I tell ya what I gonna do," Edwards said to the standing-room crowd in his thick Cajun accent. "Imma gonna give yah a parking lot." The promise for school pavement was met with ear-ringing applause. For me, it was sort of like a regular guy saying to his missus, "Honey, when I go to the grocery store, I'm going to get you some paper towels and laundry detergent." I was hoping for the promise of a real auditorium where everyone gets a comfortable seat. Nevertheless, Edwards embraced the applause and seemed to bask in it. (Today LSUS has a roomy, spacious, bed-of-roses-for-the-buttocks auditorium.)

It's easy to like Edwin Edwards. He was always a really cool guy who could adroitly tap-dance his way out of some tight places. It's just that through four terms some folks talked a lot about slick maneuvers and that R-word: racketeering. And Edwards serving himself and his many friends.

But, boy, what wit Edwards had. Like the time he faced David Duke in the 1991 runoff for governor. Edwards likened himself to Duke by saying, "We are both wizards under the sheets." The cleverness of such a remark would go unchallenged; perhaps neither its authenticity.

One very classy thing Edwards did was to offer his wife Candance a divorce so that she could begin her life anew after he headed to prison. She turned that proposal down flat, which was kinda classy, too. But the classiest thing was Edwards following through and divorcing Candance from prison. When he did that I could only compare him to Humphrey Bogart when he put Ingrid Bergman on that airplane at the end of *Casablanca*.

Treen believed the federal government doubled Edwards' sentence from the prescribed five years purely out of vindictiveness. "They didn't like him," he said. "That's not a good reason to double someone's sentence and is, I believe, a misuse of power."

When Edwards comes home in early July seeking freedom and contentment in an imperfect society, it will be a special independence day for him, wrapped most likely in a varied array of deep complex sensations that may take some time to sort out. Certainly people of sensitivity and civility hope that it is a transition of ease, hope, and happiness.

*** *On January 13, 2011, Governor Edwin Edwards left prison to complete the remaining six months of his 10-year racketeering charges in the home of his daughter, Anna. Edwards will be under home confinement until July, 2011.*

— "A Rose By Any Other Name..." —

Despite my journalistic training I never made it to Madison Avenue as an ad writer, but I did come up with the name of a championship basketball team

During my early years as a student at Louisiana Tech, Bob Haley concocted the idea of forming a basketball team to compete in the school's intramural tournament. As Bob, Butch Fincher, John David Brantly and I grouped in the confines of The Three Deuces Bar and Grill, also known as 222 Hale Hall, we sold ourselves on the brainstorm of birthing such a team. All we needed was a name. As a team member I did not score the winning basket to claim the tourney title, but did come up with a three-point name.

"What about Dunkers?" I offered. With little discussion the name was quickly adopted. I like to think that the mere name, Dunkers, paved our way to the tournament championship, but the fact is we had a pretty darn good team, one good enough to take the crown.

Reminiscing about the success of the Dunkers started me thinking about the catchy names of various products and services. Here are my choices of those I think are especially good:

Candy bar: Zagnut

Dishwashing detergent: Cascade

Automobile: Mercury Cougar

Truck: Dodge Ram

Bath soap: Zest

Soft drink: Delaware Punch

Jeans: Wrangler

Movie theater: Bijou

Toy: Slinky

Tendon: Achilles'

Ship: Argo

Artificial turf: Astroturf

Actor: Bela Lugosi

Actress: Yvonne DeCarlo

Nickname: Pecos Bill

Adopted name: Bing Crosby (b. Harry Lillis)

Meat: Bratwurst

Cheese: Roquefort

Whisky: Canadian Mist

Criminal: Caryl Chessman

Ointment: Chapstick

Ice cream treat: Eskimo Pie

Laxative: Ex-Lax

Cereal: Fruit Loops

Hand cleaner: Go-Jo

Glue: Krazy Glue

Ice cream guy: Good Humor Man

Calendar day: Groundhog Day

Bubble gum: Double Bubble

Margarine: I Can't Believe It's Not Butter

Nickname for baseball player: Wilmer "Vinegar Bend" Mizell

Nickname for football player: "Refrigerator" Perry

Baby potty: Just in Case

Hair color: Just for Men

Pantyhose: Just My Size

Verbal expression: "Jumpin' Jehoshaphat"

Nickname for basketball player: Julius "Dr. J" Erving

Pastry: Pop Tarts

Indian saying: "Kemo-sabe"

Summer house: Kennebunkport

World War II saying: "Kilroy was here."

Giant ape name: King Kong

Tissue paper: Puffs

Alien name: Klingon

TV cop: Kojak

Printing company: Kwik-Kopy

Recliner: La-Z-Boy

Super–hero disabler: Kryptonite

Laundry detergent: Cheer

Cab company: Checker

Cookies: Chips Ahoy

Race horse: Whirlaway

Cleanser: Comet

Magazine: Creative Loafing

Flooring: Congoleum

Country and western star: Conway Twitty

Beer: Busch Bavarian

Nickname for boxer: "Gentleman" Jim Corbett

Paper product: Coronet

Tool: Craftsman

Toothpaste: Gleem

Cooker: Crock-Pot

Wax paper: Cut-Rite

Music group: Third Eye Blind

Football team: 49ers

Stew: Dinty Moore

Paper cup: Dixie

Cartoon character: Elmer Fudd

Popular singer: Englebert Humperdinck

Diapers: Luvs

Nickname for dissident: Lynette "Squeaky" Fromme

Burger: Big Mac

Charcoal: Match-Light

Deodorant: Mennen Speed Stick

Pretzel: Mister Salty

Grocery store: Jitney-Jungle

Syrup: Mrs. Butterworth

Quick stop: Get N Go

Cat food: 9 Lives

Dog food: Lucky Dog

Fairy: Peaseblossom

Toy store: Toys "R" Us

Pickle: Peter Piper's pickles

Canned spaghetti: Spaghetti Os

Cigarette: Lucky Strike

Comic strip character: Smilin' Jack

Title: *Punky Brewster*

Vodka: Smirnoff

Bug killer: Raid

Name for a detective: Simon Templar

Concrete: Ready Mix

Magic word: Shazam

Artificial juice: ReaLemon

Board game: Scrabble

Nickname for golfer: "Slamming Sammy" Snead

Dishwasher: Whirlpool

Storage bags: Ziploc

Anything: Jerb

Charles Louis Tabor, Jr.
b. 1915 d. 2003

My best friend, who also happens to be my father, C.L. Tabor, Jr. died February 10, 2003. Life seemed to leave me as well, the life of writing, that is. It has been ten weeks since I last penned an article for my weekly newspaper column. But as I write this, at the beginning of a new spring, I sense rebirth, regeneration, new life.

The first thought was a memorial tribute. The problem, as I see it, is dealing with my inability to put into words what my dad meant to me. Where are those words I need to express my personal grief? Have they not yet been invented? Do such words exist? If they do, they seem just beyond my reach.

What seems to bother me most is the notion that the symbols that I ultimately settle for will not measure up, will not come close to showing the person that my father was. It is these feelings of inadequacy, I think, that has much to do with my putting off the writing of this tribute.

Perhaps I mustn't worry so much about its shortcomings. If I fall short, as I am destined to do, I must keep in mind that at any time in the future I am free to write as many tributes as I like, as often as I like, creating a series of "building blocks" whose goal is showing a true picture of who my dad was and in what way he was important, as true as I can possibly make it.

There was a time not that far distant when I believed that those who lived to the age of 87 were gifted with more than a complete and full life. Dad seemed to feel the same way; he often stated to my mother that if he could live as long as his father had lived, then he would be content with his allotment of time, which happened to add up to 87 years and 75 days. His father, C.L. Tabor, Sr., lived 87 years and 57 days. It was like Dad's wish was heard and granted.

Of course, passing away at any age is too soon. Even at 87, a relatively long life, I wasn't ready to let him go. I am sure I would feel the same if had been 97 or even 107.

A day or two after his death, I got this feeling that I would see him again. My cousin, M.L. Kilpatrick, who is also a junior, has a faith that is stronger than mine. He is certain that I will. Skeptics may find hope in the fact that a number of scientists now believe that everything in the universe is forever alive and evolving. The photons of light, for example, keep going and going and going throughout infinity. Think about this the next time you gaze at the Milky Way.

Also, consider this analogy: if you place a teaspoon of sugar into a glass of water, where does the sugar go? Does it "die"? If you allow the water to evaporate, the sugar crystals magically reappear. And through evaporation, water disappears too. But we know that it still exists in another form. Energy, as many of us know, does not die. It is merely transformed.

According to scientists Gary Schwartz, Ph.D., and Linda Russek, Ph.D., all dynamic systems, from the subatomic to the cosmic, from cells, and ideas to souls and God, have memory. Everything in the universe is alive, eternal and evolving. Every idea ever thought and every awareness ever generated is contained in the universe as information or memory; thus, consciousness survives death.

If the light of stars continue to exist forever, why not the same for loving souls? If the systemic memory hypothesis of Schwartz and Russek is true, science may some day resurrect and revise the reputation of God.

If their universal living memory process turns out to be true, scientific integrity requires that we entertain the hypothesis that not only is Dad's consciousness alive and evolving, but that he may even be part of the process of writing this book.

The Legacy of C.L. Tabor, Jr.

My most treasured item is a small, brown–grained, nondescript pocketknife that measures a mere 5 ¾ inches with its large blade open and extended. It does not have the fancy doodads of a Swiss Army knife, like magnifiers, scissors, rulers, and corkscrews. Nonetheless, I love the little knife and its plain simplicity.

It is the same knife that my father, C.L. Tabor, Jr., used when he was in his 80s to shape up a quartet of younger foul-mouths whose verbal garbage Dad felt was inappropriate in the presence of ladies, namely my mother, Grace Tabor, and her twin sister, Gladys Thompson.

I was not at the scene of the crimes, nor did Dad ever boast to me about his bringing to a halt the trashy language coming from the next booth in the restaurant. My enlightenment came years after the incident from Aunt Gladys' husband, Tommy Thompson. As Uncle Tommy related the story to me that day, Aunt Gladys nodded to verify the story's authenticity.

In short, Dad had grown impatient with the continual cussing coming from the four men seated in an adjoining restaurant booth, jumped from his nearby seat, opened the little pocketknife, pointed it at the offenders, and demanded that the dirty language cease. It did, without any rebuttal whatsoever. As I have often said, right makes might, or to appropriately update an adage, "It's not the age of the dog in the fight, but the rage of the dog in the fight."

A few months before Dad's death he came up to me, reached into his pocket, pulled out the little knife and, handing it over, declared that he was relinquishing its ownership to me, with the commandment that I, at the proper time, pass it on to my own son, Jonathan. And naturally Jonathan would be expected to bequeath the knife to his son Bailey, who is now eleven.

Perhaps this newborn ritual of handing down the knife could be carried on for the generations to come, ad infinitum.

How grand it would have been if the ritual had started in 1570 with Sir John Tabor, of Stovall, Essexshire, England, handing down the first English army knife to his son James. From second-generation James it would pass to the succeeding heirs: William of Cambridge, Thomas, Stephen of Virginia, William Sr., William Jr., John, William, Elijah of North Carolina and Union Parish Louisiana, George of Mississippi, John Burl of Union Parish, C.L. Tabor Sr. of Union and Claiborne parishes, C.L. Tabor Jr., me, Jonathan, Bailey.

Young Andrew Bailey is my only grandson, so ultimately, it will be up to him to keep his great grandfather's knife moving along in space and time. And it would be wonderful to know that future recipients might look back on my dad in somewhat the way I look back on Sir John, and, in some filiopietistic way, think of the legacy as our family's Excalibur.

– The Great Depression Hits Homer –

My dad, C.L. Tabor, Jr., was almost fourteen years old when the stock market crashed in 1929. Then it took about two years for the result of the crash to trickle down to the Deep South and Homer. That result, of course, was called the Great Depression.

Whenever Dad and my mother, Gracie Kilpatrick Tabor, spoke about this historical event, it seemed that they whispered its name in hushed tones so that "it" would not overhear them and attack again.

"Times were bad," my mother would say gravely with the rueful acceptance of a terrible knowledge, and leave it at that.

One of the most serious manifestations of the Great Depression was the loss of millions of jobs. A Homer native who lived through this time tells of three of his older brothers and a sister who had left Homer prior to the Depression and secured employment elsewhere. Through the years 1931 and 1932 all four lost their jobs and returned to Homer. Their three automobiles remained parked at their parents' home because they could not afford to buy gasoline, even though it cost about fifteen cents a gallon.

The sawmill and planer mill businesses in Homer virtually dried up. Almost all their employees were laid off. Those few who did not lose their jobs took a huge cut in pay. Families began to grow crops for the first time. Friends and neighbors traded seeds to insure variety. Families of nine shelled a bushel of black-eyed and purple-hulled peas per meal.

At sixteen, and the oldest son in his family of seven, my dad did his part to help out. A Homer eyewitness, who wishes to remain anonymous, remembers with pleasure the adventurous anticipation of his youth when he was eleven years old, watching from a small distance Dad and Larry Evans hunt rabbits near his home. The hunt began when Dad, carrying his single-shot .410 and accompanied by his "plain old" dog, hiked from his house down the tracks of the Louisiana and North West Railroad, crossing West Main Street near the old planer mill in the neighborhood of today's

Brookshire's. That's where the hunting took place: in the pastoral, verdant, unblemished woods below Larry Evans' house.

Larry Evans' "plain old" dog teamed with Dad's to chase the rabbits. And Dad and Larry Evans, their guns across their arms, waited patiently in the hush beneath the sun-shot pine trees until the rabbits circled back to them. Their "scientific" game plan provided good results. And considering their short gestation period, wild rabbits made up a flourishing population at that time.

Whenever Dad bagged a rabbit, he cut a slit between the bones of the rabbit's lower legs. Then he ran a belt that circled his midsection through the slit, and carried the rabbit around his waist. When the day was especially good, the hunters' persona became that of Hawaiian dancers adorned in raffia hula skirts.

They were not hunting for sport. "They were out to put meat on the table," my source said. It was a simple matter of survival.

Even though the Great Depression was a horrible time for folks trying to get by, there was a positive side to it.

"It brought families together," my source said.

The Mr. Gattis Pizza Lunch Bunch

The Mr. Gattis Pizza Lunch Bunch was a diverse smorgasbord of personalities and professions, including six professors in the fields of mass communications and chemistry, from two Shreveport colleges, plus an attorney, a librarian, a professional photographer, and a professional caregiver.

My informal membership with this group allowed me two hours of extemporaneous talk and laughter each Friday afternoon. Whatever the topic, whatever its flavor, we experienced, through the multiplicity of our relationships, an avenue of growth as we offered our various and conflicting prescriptions for the perfect world, sometimes running against the current of academic tradition.

We didn't consistently keep on top of the important issues in areas like politics and religion. Sometimes we gossiped; sometimes we reviewed the latest episode of *Seinfeld*. Whenever we took the path of levity, in my Friday afternoon high, I laughed at practically anything spoken.

The wonderful thing about real conversation is that it stimulates one to new insights. And always, I learned from the words of Carolyn, Chris, Ernie, Frank, Jack, LaWanda, Melly, Ron, and Suzzanne.

On one of those afternoons awhile back, the subject turned to modern youth and their willingness to take for granted the luxury of today's lifestyle.

"What they need," I said, "is a good old-fashioned depression."

A few at our dining table looked at me with horrified expressions of disapproval.

"Think of what they would learn from such an experience," I added.

I believe they would learn to:

Manage money

Appreciate having a job, any job

Work with others for a common goal

Develop survival skills

Appreciate the value of family togetherness

Become self-reliant

The First Seeds of Good

William Dean Howells offered the world some remarkably sage philosophy when he wrote that "a man never sees all that his mother has been to him until it's too late to let her know he sees it."

As my mother, Grace Kilpatrick Tabor, celebrates her birthday next Monday, I use this column to attempt to see at least some of what she been to me and to let her know about it now at this appropriate time

Most certainly I am a better person today because of my mother. In the immortal words of philosopher Immanuel Kant, "It was she who planted and nurtured the first seeds of good within me."

Even though I reached adulthood a long time ago, my mother continues to guide me down that straight path of values. Her motherly advice never offends, simply because she cleverly imparts her nuggets of wisdom with sensitively and without force. As a mother, she has the right to advise. Also because she has never realized that her adult offspring are no longer children. Her children, no matter their age, will always be her children. She said so herself.

Who exactly is my mother? Foremost, she is my No. 1 supporter, the person who has always believed in me, especially during those times when I did not believe in myself.

The angst of the down times that come from life's hard knocks melts away under the weight of her words of assuagement. Some of the chosen phrases like "God doesn't give you more than you can bear" provide strength and comfort and hope, and hearing her say them magnifies their power.

Whenever the tentacles of injustice wrap themselves around a son of hers, she, at once, metamorphoses from her usual amiable, retiring persona and turns on the transgressors with a sudden flash of defensive spirit. She is proud and honorable in this role and, during these times, I cannot help being proud of her. Almost always the villainy comes to a halt and the issue is resolved.

In 2003 when my mother became a widow after sixty-seven years of marriage, I wondered if she would crumble as a result of this traumatic life event. It didn't happen. From somewhere that perhaps only she knows, she has found strength, and has emerged as very self-reliant and independent. The emergence of this strength somewhat reminds me of that old football field adage: "When the going gets tough, the tough get going." Her own mother, Maggie Henley Kilpatrick, who was as tough as nails, was widowed in 1948 but lived independently and bravely and vigorously for another thirty-two years. I have begun to ask myself, "Do I now see some of Grandma in Mom?" If some of Grandma has become a part of Mom, then it must be recognized as sent from God. Remember, God doesn't give you more than you can bear. This is true because my mom told me so. And I would never doubt the wisdom of my mother.

Corkball Memories

One can live well without toiling, but one can not live well without leisuring....

Mortimer J. Adler, Ph.D.

When I was a teenager, I had the good fortune to be introduced to an outside game that provided for me many hours of enjoyment. It was called corkball, and it was Emory Eugene Watson and John Wayne Odom who made the introduction.

But a short time prior to my initiation I had already casually driven past Bob Haley's home on East College Street to get a fleeting glimpse of Butch Fincher and Bob swinging a wooden yardstick at an in-flight fishing cork. One of them was throwing the cork; the other was attempting to hit it with the yardstick.

At first analysis corkball seems to be fundamentally akin to baseball, for which I have an innate love. The main difference is that corkball, with little running involved, is less taxing. And here is a game that requires a limited amount of space, money, and equipment, and a small number of participants: two, three, four, perhaps more.

Basically corkball batters attempt to hit the pitcher's fastballs, curve balls, and sliders as far as possible, the greater the distance, the more valuable the hit: a prescribed number of feet for singles, additional feet for doubles, an even farther distance for triples, and the longest distance for home runs.

A large share of my early corkball time was shared with my sports-loving Uncle Hutto Tabor, who never met a game he didn't like. The two of us spent countless hours pitching and batting in our respective backyards and on the lawn of the old Claiborne Electric Co-op.

In the fall of 1958, after our high school graduation, Haley, Fincher and I took our "bats" and "balls" with us to Louisiana Tech, along with some great technical improvements for the game. For example, the fishing corks were upgraded to practice golf balls, and the yardstick bat was replaced by broom handle bats with the brush part sawed off. These changes brought us closer to the experience of throwing and hitting an actual baseball.

At Tech we recruited other Homerites to jump on the corkball bandwagon: John David Brantly, Tommy McCalman, Kenneth Gordon, Buddy Pixley, and a few Summerfield guys: Jerry Andrews, Billy Kennedy, Bill Rainach.

During Indian-summer evenings before the sun completely set, we grouped beneath the towering oaks outside Hale Hall, our dormitory, and played corkball in the presence of growing numbers of curiosity-seekers who must have wondered what in the world those visionaries from Claiborne Parish were doing now.

For the next four years we relied on a few hours of corkball to relieve the daily, torturous stress of studying. The only thing that changed were the playing fields as, through the passing semesters, we moved from dorm to dorm. And in our senior year we lost Bob Haley as a player when he left Tech for medical school. Nevertheless, corkball at Tech survived for another year.

From Homer and Ruston I took corkball to south Louisiana and introduced the game to students at LSU and Southeastern College in Hammond. On at least one occasion Butch Fincher came down to Baton Rouge and insisted that he and I play a few innings. That was the day he hit about ten home runs off me.

When I returned home to north Louisiana, new Shreveport friends like Charlie "Glazed Donut" Johnson, Jimmy "Tick Tock" Bates, Conway Link, James Moore, Ed Wiley and Robin Young came to know corkball. And my son Jonathan, too.

Other Homer people that I have enjoyed the game of corkball with include G.W. Zachary, Key Fincher, Billy Boyd, Duvalle McCalman ,George McCalman, Don McCalman, Ed Foster, David Tooke and Chuck Talley.

And on one special day during a work break a number of years back, I tossed a few corkballs at my dad. I was really surprised at how he, broomstick in hand, hit one line drive after another. As far as I know, he had never played before and never played after that time. But I am glad that Dad and I had that one corkball moment.

Today, as I find myself near my dad's age when he smacked those line drives in a hay-filled barn, I realize that that I have possibly experienced my final corkball moment. But I retain so many pleasant memories that they seem to blend into a kaleidoscope of various "bases-loaded" strikeouts, and grand-slam home runs onto the roof of the old two-story McCalman house on Dutchtown Road, and leaping catches of fly balls at close quarters to home run markers like half-grown sycamores or flowering dogwood trees.

Philosopher Mortimer J. Adler knew the importance of this kind of play for the human spirit. He said that the purpose of play "being pleasure and pleasure being one of the real goods that enrich a human life and contribute to happiness, it would appear to follow that we are under some obligation to play and amuse ourselves in our pursuit of happiness or in our effort to make a good human life for ourselves."

Eating Up Golf

When I retired from LSUS in May of 2001 I also retired from the game of golf, sold my clubs, and decided to eat and read for the rest of my life. I did not think quitting golf was that difficult until I saw in Barnes and Noble the other day a book on how to give up golf. A book on giving up smoking or loafing I can understand. But golf? What I needed was a really good book on giving up eating.

Some time ago I began to reconsider my decision when Bob Haley, who introduced me to the maddening game in the 1960s, invited me to play a round with him and Butch Fincher. I agreed to join them at the Homer Country Club course as a non-active spectator and also accepted their invitation for lunch as a fully active participant. Eating food is much easier than hitting a golf ball

Watching Bob and Butch play so well brought back some good memories of the days I shot bogey golf. My decision to come out of golf retirement was pretty much solidified a few days later when my son Jonathan said he had ordered new clubs for my birthday. I suspect that Bob, Butch, and Jonathan look forward to hammering me into the fairways.

I realize that I have a ways to go to get back to my earlier level, mainly because my thoughts the past few years have been more on the U.S. Open-Face. In the world of golf, the phrase, "Let the big dog eat" means to swing away with the driver. For example, a golfer might say, "Number 12 is a long par five but it is wide open, so you can let the big dog eat." For me, it was "Let the big hog eat."

Here's how bad it has been:

I left the driving range for a kitchen range.

A foursome was a meal with three other eaters who shared my appreciation for food.

A four-ball match became a four-course meal.

"Green fees" paid for cans of turnip and mustard greens.

No matter the weather, the links were always hot because they came from Stateline Barbecue down the road from my house in Bethany.

Before I took a mulligan, I made sure it had plenty of squirrel meat.

Drives were to restaurants, whose ratings were more important than those of golf courses.

Instead of commanding a Titleist to bite, I commanded my jaws to bite.

The Noodle golf ball was replaced by chicken noodle soup.

The blade of a butcher knife replaced that of a five iron.

The sweet spot was the center of a jelly roll, which along with the dinner roll, replaced the roll of a wedge shot.

The cute dimples of the Pillsbury Dough Boy were favored over those of a golf ball.

Bogey was the star of *Casablanca*, which I watched with a nearby TV tray packed with pizzas.

Getting into roughage was much more simple than getting out of the rough.

When a pitch shot is hit a much shorter distance than intended, it is called a chili dip. My chili dips were scooped by the curl of a large Frito.

Sinking a donut in a cup of java replaced sinking a ball in the number nine cup.

I frequently asked if there was a turkey leg left rather than a dog leg to the left.

Improving my recipes was more important than improving my lies.

I favored drumsticks over flagsticks, and the duck soup over the duck hook.

Instead of hitting a Maxfli nestled in fluffy grass, I decorated cakes with Nestle's fluffy frosting.

A ball buried halfway in a sand bunker had a fried egg look.

Fried gator I preferred to a gator grip.

I used the word *gimmie* only in sentences like, "Gimmie some of that gravy."

Pin sheet became a cookie sheet.

Pot roast replaced pot bunker.

"Scramble" was my order to whoever was doing my eggs.

Short cake was more interesting than short game.

But now...

Now that golf is again a part of my life, I will adhere to the following affirmations:

Eat less food, play more golf.

Lose ten pounds, lose ten strokes.

Reduce the waistline, reduce the handicap.

Shoot par golf, fly to the moon.

Only The Good Die Young (December 5, 2002)

It's that time again. The semi-annual visit to the dentist. Monday, 2 p.m. Six months ago I wrote the date on the calendar, so I can't say that I forgot. Even if I were to forget, those nice ladies at Dr. Everitt's Shreveport office on Mackey Lane will call to make sure that I show up. So, there's no escape. No excuses.

With their imaginations in overdrive, people waste a lot of time thinking up some really creative excuses to avoid going to the dentist. For example, they think because they floss on a regular basis they don't need to go. And just days ago a friend of mine said he's not going until they wrap up that dreadful case about the AIDS-infected dentist in Florida, which, you may remember, was a long time ago.

The best excuse I ever heard was conjured up by my pal Luke. He says that his dog Spider doesn't go to the dentist and his teeth are fine. So Luke wonders why *he* has to go.

Although Dr. Everitt is nearing retirement, I haven't been seeing him that long. There's a sad reason I'm seeing him at all. His younger partner, Dr. Jack Witte, had been my dentist for some time. I hesitate to call Witte a nice guy because *nice* is so general and vague. Nonetheless, whatever *nice* encompasses, it certainly defines Witte. Being the occupant of the dentist chair doesn't allow the patient much talk time, so while there, I mostly listened and Witte talked away. He was a good talker, covering topics like his Fair Park High School days when he had as a teacher a good friend of mine from college, James McElroy.

From there, Witte might carry his talk from prep school to Louisiana Tech, where he quarterbacked the Bulldog football team. And he was especially proud of his involvement in the Fellowship of Christian Athletes. And, most important for him, his wife and three kids.

Knowing stuff like this creates a bond. And when that bond is broken, it hurts.

The last time I was in Witte's chair, on November 30, 2000, he seemed different. Aloof maybe, like his mind was light years away. Or maybe sullen. I was hard to tell what it was because he didn't talk much that day. I started thinking crazy thoughts like maybe he was unhappy about the balance due on my two root canals that the insurance company was slow in paying.

After Witte was done with me, I stopped by the business area to set up my next appointment. Witte, perhaps sensing my concern, came by and put his hand on my shoulder as a way of saying that whatever was bothering him was okay as far as he was concerned, and I guess to say goodbye.

"I'll see you in May," I said cheerfully, although he probably guessed at that moment I wouldn't. Five months later, the second week of May, his funeral was held. Pancreatic cancer. Forty-five years old. Much too young to die.

Finding out about Witte's death via a newspaper obituary was beyond shocking. Seems that he had not told any of his patients. Yet he continued to serve them. Those who saw him over the next several weeks knew something was wrong because he began to lose so much weight. That dreadful, slow change I did not see because he had just gotten the bad news shortly before my last visit with him. Yet, he continued to work full time for as long as he could, then part time as much as he could, then not at all.

When I went in for my appointment just days after the funeral, the dental office, with pictures of Witte's family still there, was like a tomb. People quietly did their professional duties, office personnel scheduled appointments, hygienists did the preliminaries, Dr. Everitt tended to teeth and gums. Their bodies moved silently through space and time; their hearts and minds were with Witte.

At the end Witte was philosophical. "God has other work for me," he declared.

Billy Joel's song is right. Only the good die young.

SHHH, I'm Hard of Hearing

All my life I have had difficulty converting spoken sounds into meaningful words, been the butt of thousands of jokes and disparaging remarks from friends, family, colleagues, and even students in my classroom.

When I was a kid, watching movies at the old Pelican Theater in Homer, cowboy "Wild Bill" Elliott often told his adversaries in black hats, "I'm a peaceable man." But for thirteen years and through approximately ninety B-westerns I heard him say, "I'm a piece of a man." I tried hard to make sense out of what I thought must be some sort of frontier riddle. Finally, somebody with normal hearing set me straight, with a little ridicule thrown in as the cost for the enlightenment.

My Grandfather Tabor, who was a little hard-of-hearing himself, did not accept my handicap. He felt that I heard what I wanted to hear and paid no mind to what did not interest me. He attempted to prove his belief by whispering to me at family get-togethers, "Ice cream," then asking me what he had just said. Amazingly, I answered correctly, not understanding at the time that I was reading his lips, a talent that I unconsciously developed over time.

For some reason some ordinarily nice people with twenty-twenty hearing seem to be more accepting of the lame and the blind, but when their mumblings are not completely understood, their patience takes a holiday. One of their favorite phrases when they are asked to repeat something, and one that I hate to hear, is: "Never mind." Comes across as a bit insulting.

In 2002 I became aware of an excellent support group that tries to raise public awareness about those with hearing loss. At that time, it was known as SHHH (Self-Help for Hard of Hearing People). In November of 2005 the name was changed to Hearing Loss Association of America. This organization does a lot more in addition to sensitizing the general public about the needs of people who are hard of hearing. It provides adults and children with tools for self help; promotes understanding of the nature, causes, complications, and remedies of hearing loss; and promotes medical research and new technology like assistive listening devices.

These devices have made great strides. When I attended my first SHHH meeting, I was outfitted with a lightweight, wireless headset that utilized an infrared listening system. It was marvelous. Like getting the ears you didn't get at birth. As I listened to the guest speaker, I did not miss a single word.

Through the headset I heard crisp, clear words, without the distractions of unwanted noise that I got with hearing aids. When the meeting was over, I didn't want to give up the headset.

For years I denied my hearing loss. After all, I was only a kid. Only old people couldn't hear. So, for too many years of school I sat in the back of the classroom and daydreamed my way to making D's. Then I realized that if I was not to waste my Dad's money by getting kicked out of college, something had to be done.

The first step was to ask my Louisiana Tech professors who had seating charts to make an exception and put me as close as possible to their lecterns. Fortunately, they all agreed to do so.

This worked fairly well for four years until I found myself on the speaker's side of the lectern. My high school and college students had no trouble hearing me, but I had trouble hearing them.

The next step was accepting the $300 that my mother gave me for my first hearing aid. This improved the situation, but the device finally wore out. By the time I was ready for a new hearing aid, the price had jumped to $500. By then I could make the payment myself, but Hearing Aid Number Two eventually broke down as well. When I went to get Number Three, I came home with twins. The hearing aid woman at Highland Medical Center in Shreveport convinced me that I would double my pleasure by wearing one in each ear. She was right. Thus, my right ear jumped on board after years of neglect.

Hearing aids are far from perfect. At social gatherings and the like, the pain of shrill, unwanted sound is worse than not hearing. So I usually picked my spots for wearing them: always the classrooms and important meetings, and sometimes at the movies.

My hearing loss is complicated by the fact that I also have *recruitment*, an incurable condition that causes an exaggerated sound even though there is only a small increase in noise level. With recruitment there is a perceived loudness for sounds in a certain pitch region. At one point I cannot hear the sound because of the hearing loss in that frequency, then when the sound reaches a certain loudness and/or frequency, I am blown away because I perceive it as far too loud. It can be something as simple as someone coughing.

When someone is talking to me, knowing of my hearing loss, he may raise his voice slightly, and I might say, "Don't shout," or "SHHH, I'm hard of hearing, but you don't have to yell!"

Many people have no trouble understanding hearing loss, but have difficulty understanding recruitment. Recruitment simply allows a smaller window for acceptable sounds. Outside the window on one side, the sufferer cannot make words out of sounds; outside the window on the other side, the sufferer winces in pain. Some things that especially give me trouble are the sounds of sneakers scrapping across a floor and the loading of a dishwasher. Strangely, I'm not annoyed by the sound if I make it myself. This is quite typical, though.

Other than using assistive listening devices, reading lips, and being involved with support groups, about the only thing I can do about my hearing loss is to simply accept it and try to adapt to living with it. A very good coping technique is to find humor in the situations these disorders produce. Rather than be frustrated, I try to smile when an incident such as the following occurs:

When I taught at LSU in Shreveport, I sometimes chatted informally with students after classes were done for the day. One day after the last class of the semester one of my favorite students, Jerry Scott, sat down next to me in the editing lab. Jerry, a burly African-American a little on the heavy side, seemed to enjoy discussing social and political issues with me. He became a journalist with *The* (Shreveport) *Times* for awhile. He usually signaled his desire for discussion with the lead-in, "You know…"

"You know, Mr. Tabor," he said that day, "I don't understand all the fuss over the Confederate flag."

"Well, Jerry," I replied, "flags are symbols like words. And you know that words themselves are harmless. It's the meaning that we attach to the symbols that gives them power. But we have the power within ourselves to decide that they are harmless. Really, people choose to emotionally react to these symbols."

"Kinda like 'sticks and stones…'"

"Exactly, Jerry."

Later, I moved the topic to the upcoming final exams. "Jerry, are you ready to do some heavy studying for finals?"

"You know, Mr. Tabor, I do my best studying when I haven't had any."

At least that's what I thought he said.

I was somewhat surprised at his remark. Jerry just didn't seem the type. I had never seen him even talking to a girl. "Interesting," I said, thinking that perhaps I could get a federal grant to research this phenomenon.

The next day I popped into the office of my department chairman, Dr. Jack Nolan, a transplant from Binghamton, New York. We were wrapping up some last-minute business for the semester. As our work began to get finished up, I remembered my conversation with Jerry.

"Jack, I heard a rather interesting remark from Jerry Scott yesterday."

Nolan's interest shot up. He was fond of Jerry, too. So I proceeded to tell him.

First Nolan looked a bit puzzled. Then the corners of his mouth lifted a little. Then he grinned.

Then he laughed.

"John, you need to get those hearing aids checked out. Earlier this morning Jerry and I were discussing techniques for studying. What he said to you was this: 'I do my best studying when I have a headache.'"

I allowed this corrected version to sink in and thought for a moment.

"That's interesting, too," I replied, thinking that perhaps I could get a federal grant to research this phenomenon.

It was Nolan who, in 1996 or thereabout, beefed up my personal Sinatra collection by taping tons of Frank's songs for me, including my favorites: *I've Got You Under My Skin* and *Strangers in the Night*. It was not that hard to do. Jack simply made use of the Nolan Museum of Music, which was in his home, where the walls were covered with thousands of CDs, mostly jazz.

Whenever Jack received his monthly LSUS paycheck he bought CDs, and if any money was left, he bought food for his wife, Chris.

I wrote the following on the last birthday that my father lived to celebrate, November 27, 2002:

————————— November 27, 1915 —————————

At the age of eighty-seven, Mary Baker Eddy founded *The Christian Science Monitor* newspaper, Sophocles wrote the play *Philoctetes*, John Gielgud appeared in the film *Prospero's Books*, and American pathologist Francis Peyton Rous won the Nobel Prize for chemistry.

Today (Nov. 27) my dad, C.L. Tabor Jr. joins this elite group by celebrating his 87th birthday. He did some great things, too. If not for my dad, I would not be writing this column. For more years than I can remember, he worked seven days a week in dusty oil fields so that I could get the college education that he didn't. If I did not fathom in the fifties and sixties that this was a special gift effected through personal sacrifice, then I do now.

As I was growing up, I didn't hunt quail with him as much as maybe he would have liked, but occasionally we got through the boundaries of time and distance and had our moments. Like when he was forty-seven and we worked on an oil derrick together in the boonies between Homer and Ruston. It was a one-night, one-time job for me, filling in for somebody, but the event made a lasting impression. I marveled at how he and his fellow roughnecks moved in unison and precision beneath the towering, god-like derrick, constantly positioning oil pipes, going non-stop without even a supper break. Those men ate on the run.

When he was sixty-seven we hooked up again, painting the house of Matilda Calendar Langhill one summer day. This time we took a lunch break from the heat, traveling the fraction of a mile to devour Mom's excellent home cooking of corn on the cob, black–eyed peas, cornbread, and squash, along with fresh sliced tomatoes, and iced tea to wash all that down.

Since those days he has slowed down a bit, trading in his steel hat and painter's cap for a lawn chair so that he can sit peacefully in the front yard and keep tabs on the goings-on across the street at Claiborne Electric.

One thing did not change as he aged. His macho stubbornness. Last Fourth of July while replacing a ceiling light bulb, he slipped and fell, gashing his right arm. He did his best to keep this accident a secret, but a blood-soaked towel was the tell–tale clue. Roping and tying a young, untamed steer is an easier task than getting my dad to a hospital, but fortunately the task was accomplished. Dr. Haynes sewed him up and gave him a tetanus shot and that arm was ready for more things to do around the house.

I aspire to develop just a fraction of my dad's class and character. As long as you have those attributes, you don't have to establish a newspaper, or write a play, or be a great actor, or even win the Nobel Prize. Today it is time to award my Dad an unnamed, mythical prize for successfully performing with dignity his duties as a father, and for enduring for eighty-seven birthdays.

Happy birthday, Dad. This one's for you:

I just got time for one more round,
Set 'em up, my friends,
Then I'll be gone
Then you can let some other fool sit down.
Pop a top again.

Read a Good Book Lately?

When I was just frying size one of my biggest Saturday morning thrills in the late forties and early fifties was visiting the Claiborne Parish Library on the second floor of the city hall building, where I was engulfed with the wonderful, mixed smells of paper, ink, and cloth. I found it difficult to believe that I could tote home an armload of books for a couple of weeks at absolutely no cost. Of course if I went past the fourteen-day loan period without renewing those treasures, I was assessed a hefty fine of two cents. In those days the money for a three-day fine could buy a 6 ½ ounce Coke and a package of peanut butter and molasses Kits at Gill's Grocery Store.

The trigger for my learning to read was newspaper comic strips and miniature magazines that we called funny books, whether the fare between the covers was funny or not. By studying each cartoon panel and analyzing the words in the speech balloons hovering over the comic characters' heads I gradually began to make sense out of what first looked like hieroglyphics. Thus, these self-teaching experiences jump-started my learning to read at the Homer Grammar School.

In my early teens I significantly matured as a reader when I recognized that the premier issue of *MAD* comic book was something special. Right away I handed my dime to Mrs. Schultz and devoured the historic premier issue. When I reached my thirties, I put aside *MAD*, which had become a magazine, and began reading books again. At first almost anything, even Mickey Spillane private eye novels. How smug I felt, reading great literature.

Then two somewhat dramatic things happened. First, I got my hands on James McCalman's copy of Clifton Fadiman's *The Lifetime Reading Plan,* in which Fadiman suggests a list of one hundred essential readings to bring about enlargement, self-enhancement, and self-discovery. Anyone who thinks that a lifetime is more than enough to churn through a mere one hundred selections, should consider that ONE of Fadiman's selections alone is the complete works of William Shakespeare. Fadiman warns in his preliminary "Talk With the Reader" in the book's early pages that the one hundred selections may take fifty years to finish. Maybe more, maybe less. The point is that the readings are intended to be an important part of a whole life, no matter what one's present age may be.

Second, in the mid eighties I was busy reading through the one hundred selections when Pat Turnley, a voracious reader, suggested that he and I team with our friend John Turner to form a reading group. The idea was to read a book each month and discuss it following a gourmet meal. Good food and good books, of course, "are to be tasted...swallowed...and chewed and digested." We named the club MAPS, an acronym for the Mortimer Adler Philosophical Society, in honor of the co-author of *How to Read a Book*, a tome similar to Fadiman's. Adler wrote volumes of philosophical books, including *Six Great Ideas,* and *How to Think About God.*

The subtitle for *How to Read a Book* is *The Classic Guide to Intelligent Reading.* The quantity of Adler's suggested selections exceeds that of Fadiman's, and many of his choices duplicate Fadiman's. One that does not is the Old Testament, number two on his lengthy list.

One might find some of Adler's picks somewhat challenging. All of us, at one time or another, have struggled with a difficult book. Don't give up on such a book. Understanding just half of a really tough book, Adler believed, is much better than not understanding at all. Subsequent readings of the book will increase the level of comprehension. Good books that are over your head, Adler believed, "would not be good for you if they were not." So read them anyway and pull yourself up to their level. One way to do this is by "coming to terms" with a book's author by interpreting and understanding his or her key words.

MAPS, formed in 1986, grew through the nineties up to ten members, but no more, because it was felt that a number above that might defeat the group's purpose. During MAPS' active years (1986-2000) I noticed that others were starting reading groups. Also, books about creating such organizations were popping up all over.

Here are some affordable paperbacks that tell how to start a reading group, how to choose members, how to lead well-balanced discussions, what kind of rules to put in place, and most importantly, what to read:

The Book Group Book, by Ellen Slezak

The Complete Idiot's Guide to Starting a Reading Group, by Patrick Sauer

The New York Public Library Guide to Reading Groups, by Rollen Saal

The Reading Group Book, by David Laskin and Holly Hughes

The Reading Group Handbook, by Rachel W. Jacobsohn

What to Read, by Mickey Pearlman

And of course:

The Lifetime Reading Plan, by Clifton Fadiman

How to Read a Book, by Mortimer J. Adler and Charles Van Doren

Whether you succeed in launching your own group or go solo as I have done from time to time, you have an opportunity to change and grow and enrich your life. After years of reading the great books you will literally be a new person.

When MAPS had covered one hundred selections, I polled the members to determine the most popular reads. I presented them with the following letter:

Dear MAPS member,

Please select your top ten selections/works by using ORDINAL numbers such as 1st, 2nd, 3rd, 4th, etc. to indicate your selections. First-place choices will be assigned ten points each, second-place choices nine points each, third-place choices eight points each, etc. Totals will be calculated and a cumulative consensus top ten list will be determined by largest point totals.

For myself, I plan to make choices based on intangibles such as each selection's characterization, its enlightenment, entertainment value, personal impact, importance, literary merit, quality and style, meaningfulness, novelty, plot (fiction), profundity, readability, revelations, its ability to change my life, and simply its giving a good overall feeling and sense of wonder.

John

Here are the final rankings:

1. *Angela's Ashes,* Frank McCourt (49 points)
2. *Dead Man Walking,* Helen Prejean (33 points)
3. *Cosmos,* Carl Sagan (25 points)
   Into Thin Air, Jon Krakauer (25 points)
5. *Midnight in the Garden of Good and Evil,* John Berendt (24 points)
6. *Cold Mountain,* Charles Frazier (19 points)
   The Great Gatsby, F. Scott Fitzgerald (19 points).
8. *Rising Tide,* John M. Barry (17 points)
   Sophie's World, Jostein Gaarder (17 points)
10. *The Hot Zone,* Richard Preston (16 points)
    Six Great Ideas, Mortimer J. Adler (16 points)
    Undaunted Courage, Stephen E. Ambrose (16 points)

HONORABLE MENTION

13. *The Hobbit,* J.R.R. Tolkien (14 points)
    The Power and the Glory, Graham Greene (14 points)
15. *A Brief History of Time,* Stephen W. Hawking (13 points)
    The Perfect Storm, Sebastian Junger (13 points)
17. *The Double Helix,* James D. Watson (10 points)
18. *The Shipping News,* E. Annie Proulx (9 points)
    The Vigilante Committees of the Attakapas, Alexandre Barde (9 points)
20. *What Do YOU Care What Other People Think?,* Richard P. Feynman (8 points)
21. *Plain and Simple,* Sue Bender (7 points)
22. *A Prayer for Owen Meany,* John Irving (6 points)
23. *The Bell Curve,* Richard J. Herrnstein and Charles Murray (5 points)
    The Republic, Plato (5 points)
    The True Believer, Eric Hoffer (5 points)
    Tuesdays With Morrie, Mitch Albom (5 points)
27. *Come Back to the Farm,* Jesse Stuart (4 points)

Mind Hunter, John Douglas and Mark Olshaker (4 points)

The Prince, Machiavelli (4 points)

The Science of God, Gerald L. Schroeder (4 points)

31 *Introductory Lectures on Psychoanalysis*, Sigmund Freud (3 points)

Pale Blue Dot, Carl Sagan (3 points)

33.*Gorgias*, Plato (2 points)

Men are from Mars, Women are from Venus, John Gray (2 points)

Origins, Robert Shapiro (2 points)

36.*The Angels and Us*, Mortimer J. Adler (1 point)

Huey Long, T. Harry Williams (1 point)

Manufacturing Consent, Edward S. Herman and Noam Chomsky (1 point)

The following selections did not receive any top ten votes:

How to Read a Book, Mortimer J. Adler and Charles Van Doren

The Origin of the Species, Charles Darwin

The Difference of Man and the Difference it Makes, Mortimer J. Adler

Aristotle for Everybody, Mortimer J. Adler

The Paideia Program, Mortimer J. Adler

Crito, Plato

Socrates' Defense (Apology), Plato

The Varieties of Religious Experience, William James

Why I Am Not a Christian, Bertrand Russell

Walden, Henry David Thoreau

Pygmalion, Bernard Shaw

The Universe and Dr. Einstein, Lincoln Barnett

Black Like Me, John Howard Griffin

How to Think About God, Mortimer J. Adler

How to Speak, How to Listen, Mortimer J. Adler

Spring Moon, Bette Bao Lord

The Elephant Man, Ashley Montagu

Absalom, Absalom!, William Faulkner

All the President's Men, Carl Bernstein and Bob Woodward

Rules for the Direction of the Mind, Rene Descartes

The Scientific Outlook, Bertrand Russell

The Interpretation of Dreams, Sigmund Freud

Caveat, Alexander M. Haig, Jr.

From the Old Testament: *Genesis, Exodus, Leviticus, Numbers,* and *Deuteronomy*

New Essays on the Human Understanding, Leibniz

Tartuffe, Moliere

Death of a Salesman, Arthur Miller

When Bad Things Happen to Good People, Harold S. Kushner

Democracy in America, Alexis De Tocqueville

Antigone, Sophocles

The Tragedy of Romeo and Juliet, William Shakespeare

Mother Angelica's Answers, Not Promises, Mother M. Angelica

The Iliad, Homer

The Odyssey, Homer

Huckleberry Finn, Mark Twain

Parliament of Whores, P.J. O'Rourke

The Descent of Man, Charles Darwin

Learned Optimism, Martin E.P. Seligman

Awakenings, Oliver Sacks

Jazz, Toni Morrison

Hamlet, William Shakespeare

The Power of Myth, Joseph Campbell

Tom Jones, Henry Fielding

The Medusa and the Snail, Lewis Thomas

God and the New Physics, Paul Davies

Harvey Penick's Little Red Book, Harvey Penick

The Neon Rain, James Lee Burke

National Geographic magazine article, "Quiet Miracles of the Brain," (June 1995)

Meditations on First Philosophy, Rene Descartes

Murder, No Doubt, Ruth Langlos

Native Tongue, Carl Hiaasen

Emotional Intelligence, Daniel Goleman

If…(Questions for the Game of Life), Evelyn McFarlane and James Saywell

The Giver, Lois Lowry

The Atheist Syndrome, John P. Koster, Jr.

Are You a Conservative or a Liberal?, Bradley Leary and Victor Kamber

At Home, Gore Vidal

In The Lion's Den, Nina Shea

One Hundred Years of Solitude, Gabriel Garcia Marquez

The Demon-Haunted World, Carl Sagan

Life magazine special issue on the millennium (Fall 1997)

Half Asleep in Frog Pajamas, Tom Robbins

How the Irish Saved Civilization, Thomas Cahill

The Screwtape Letters, C.S. Lewis

In addition to *Angela's Ashes* the following were number one picks: *The Hobbit, Cold Mountain, Into Thin Air, The Double Helix, The Power and the Glory,* and *Six Great Ideas.* Quite diverse!

My own top ten choices were:

1. *Into Thin Air*
2. *Angela's Ashes*
3. *Cosmos*
4. *The Shipping News*
5. *The Perfect Storm*
6. *The Great Gatsby*
7. *Come Back to the Farm*
8. *Introductory Lectures on Psychoanalysis*
9. *The Republic*
10. *Rising Tide*

Following the survey MAPS made the following selections: *A Lesson Before Dying,* Ernest J. Gaines; *Why Christianity Must Change Or Die,* John Shelby Spong; *Of Human Bondage,* W. Somerset Maugham; *Building a Bridge to the Eighteenth Century,* Neil Postman; *Team Rodent,* Carl Hiaasen; *'Tis,* Frank McCourt; *Crime and Punishment,* Fyodor Dostoevsky; *The Good Earth,* Pearl S. Buck; *Louisiana Power and Light,* John Dufresne.

When MAPS disbanded circa 2000, I focused on a different reading agenda. I decided to read all the Pulitzer Prize winners in literature beginning with the first winner in 1918 and moving in chronological fashion so that I could get a sense of how American literary fiction has evolved through the years.

To achieve the utmost diversity in reading good fiction, I later decided to include other prize winners as well: National Book Award, Pen/Faulkner Award, the Howells Medal, the *Los Angeles Times* Book Prize, the National Book Critics Circle Award, and the Bellwether Prize.

The PEN/Faulkner provides three American writers the opportunity to honor their fellow writers by being judges. This award, revived in 1980, was started by William Faulkner with his 1949 Nobel Prize money.

The *Los Angeles Times* Book Prize winner is determined by three judges chosen by the newspaper. The award seems to favor writings about characters who attempt to free themselves from psychological or political oppression.

The National Book Award winners capture national challenges and contemporary life.

The Critics Circle is made up of almost six hundred book review editors and professional book critics.

The Pulitzer recognizes works that include mostly tragic themes in American life. Newspaper publisher Joseph Pulitzer established the prize, which was first awarded in 1918.

The Bellwether Prize for Fiction is given to a previously unpublished novel that supports literature of social change and issues of social justice. It was established in 2000 by author Barbara Kingsolver.

Thus far, I have read through fifty-five Pulitzer, twenty-four National Book Award, nine Howells, five NBCCA, and two PEN/Faulkner winners, sometimes a bit off kilter on the strict chronology.

Without going into a detailed analysis I have ranked those readings in the following order:

THE PULITZER PRIZE FOR LITERATURE

1. *Rabbit is Rich*, John Updike (1982)
2. *Rabbit at Rest*, John Updike (1991)
3. *The Grapes of Wrath*, John Steinbeck (1940)
4. *Dragon's Teeth*, Upton Sinclair (1943)
5. *The Confessions of Nat Turner*, William Styron (1968)
6. *The Caine Mutiny*, Herman Wouk (1952)
7. *The Store*, T.S. Stribling (1933)
8. *The Good Earth*, Pearl S. Buck (1932)
9. *Gone With the Wind*, Margaret Mitchell (1937)
10. *Arrowsmith*, Sinclair Lewis (1926)
11. *Lonesome Dove*, Larry McMurtry (1986)
12. *Advise and Consent*, Allen Drury (1960)
13. *The Shipping News*, E. Annie Proulx (1994)
14. *The Amazing Adventures of Kavalier and Clay*, Michael Chabon (2001)
15. *Tales of the South Pacific*, James A. Michener (1948)
16. *The Travels of Jaimie McPheeters*, Robert Lewis Taylor (1959)
17. *The Fixer*, Bernard Malamud (1967)
18. *The Way West*, A.B. Guthrie, Jr. (1950)
19. *Andersonville*, MacKinlay Kantor (1956)
20. *A Bell for Adano*, John Hersey (1945)
21. *All the King's Men*, Robert Penn Warren (1947)
22. *The Edge of Sadness*, Edwin O'Connor, (1962)
23. *The Reivers*, William Faulkner (1963)
24. *To Kill a Mockingbird*, Harper Lee (1961)
25. *So Big*, Edna Ferber (1925)
26. *The Age of Innocence*, Edith Wharton (1921)
27. *A Summons to Memphis*, Peter Taylor (1987)
28. *A Confederacy of Dunces*, John Kennedy Toole (1981)
29. *The Old Man and the Sea*, Ernest Hemingway (1953)
30. *Journey in the Dark*, Martin Flavin (1944)
31. *The Magnificent Ambersons*, Booth Tarkington (1919)
32. *Laughing Boy*, Oliver LaFarge (1930)

33. *Guard of Honor*, James Gould Cozzens (1949)

34. *Scarlet Sister Mary*, Julia Peterkin (1929)

35. *His Family*, Ernest Poole (1918)

36. *The Bridge of San Luis Rey*, Thorton Wilder (1928)

37. *The Yearling*, Marjorie Kinnan Rawlings (1939)

38. *Alice Adams*, Booth Tarkington (1922)

39. *A Death in the Family*, James Agee (1958)

40. *The Keepers of the House*, Shirley Ann Grau (1965)

41. *Honey in the Horn*, Harold L. Davis (1936)

42. *Now in November*, Josephine Winslow Johnson (1935)

43. *Early Autumn*, Louis Bromfield (1927)

44. *The Able McLaughlins*, Margaret Wilson (1924)

45. *In This Our Life*, Ellen Glasgow (1942)

46. *Years of Grace*, Margaret Ayer Barnes (1931)

47. *The Optimist's Daughter*, Eudora Welty (1973)

48. *Interpreter of Maladies*, Jhumpa Lahiri (2000)

49. *The Stone Diaries*, Carol Shields (1995)

50. *Lamb in His Bosom*, Caroline Miller (1934)

51. *The Late George Apley*, John Phillips Marquand (1938)

52. *House Made of Dawn*, N. Scott Momaday (1969)

53. *One of Ours*, Willa Cather (1923)

54. *The Town*, Conrad Richter (1951)

55. *A Fable*, William Faulkner (1955)

THE NATIONAL BOOK AWARD

1. *Rabbit is Rich*, John Updike (1982)

2. *The Magic Barrel*, Bernard Malamud (1959)

3. *Sophie's Choice*, William Styron (1980)

4. *From Here to Eternity*, James Jones (1952)

5. *The Shipping News*, E. Annie Proulx (1993)

6. *The Fixer*, Bernard Malamud (1967)

7. *The Man With the Golden Arm*, Nelson Algren (1950)

8. *Ten North Frederick*, John O'Hara (1956)

9. *The Centaur*, John Updike (1964)

10. *The Echo Maker*, Richard Powers (2006)

11. *Morte D'Urban*, J.F. Powers, (1963)

12. *Goodbye, Columbus*, Philip Roth (1960)

13. *The Spectator Bird*, Wallace Stegner (1977)

14. *Herzog*, Saul Bellow (1965)

15. *The Wapshot Chronicle*, John Cheever (1958)

16. *The Adventures of Augie March*, Saul Bellow (1954)

17. *Cold Mountain*, Charles Frazier (1997)

18. *Invisible Man*, Ralph Ellison (1953)

19. *The Moviegoer*, Walker Percy (1962)

20. *The Waters of Kronos*, Conrad Richter (1961)

21. *The Collected Stories of William Faulkner*, William Faulkner (1951)

22. *The Field of Vision*, Wright Morris (1957)

23. *Steps*, Jerzy Kosinski (1969)

24. *A Fable*, William Faulkner (1955)

THE HOWELLS MEDAL

1. *Rabbit at Rest*, John Updike (1995)

2. *The Confessions of Nat Turner*, William Styron (1970)

3. *The Good Earth*, Pearl S. Buck (1935)

4. *Underworld*, Don DeLillo (2000)

5. *The Wapshot Scandal*, John Cheever (1965)

6. *Billy Bathgate*, E.L. Doctorow (1990)

7. *Death Comes for the Archbishop*, Willa Cather (1930)

8. *By Love Possessed*, James Gould Cozzens (1960)

9. *The Ponder Heart*, Eudora Welty (1955)

NATIONAL BOOK CRITICS CIRCLE AWARD

1. *Rabbit is Rich*, John Updike (1981)

2. *Rabbit at Rest*, John Updike (1990)

3. *A Lesson Before Dying*, Earnest J. Gaines (1993)

4. *Billy Bathgate*, E.L. Doctorow (1989)

5. *The Stone Diaries*, Carol Shields (1994)

PEN/FAULKNER AWARD

1. *Bel Canto*, Ann Patchett (2002)
2. *Billy Bathgate*, E.L. Doctorow (1990)

A Memorial

Remember how short my time is.

Psalms 89:47

Paul Brown of Haynesville died at the age of 31 after suffering severe brain damage in a motorcycle accident at the age of 16.

Phillip "Butch" Chadwick died in Homer from a self-inflicted gunshot wound on February 23, 1978. He was 38.

Gladney Davidson died in an automobile accident in Atlanta, Georgia.

Kenneth Gordon died at the age of 71 from cancer.

Coach Glenn Gossett died from complications of Alzheimer's disease.

Bill James died in a one-car automobile accident between Homer and Minden.

Pat Larkin died from self-strangulation in his Shreveport, Louisiana apartment.

Coach Bill May died from complications of Parkinson's disease. He was 80.

John Wayne Odom died from diabetes.

Billy Charles Windsor died from cancer at the age of 50.

Harry Francis Willard, a.k.a. Willard the Wizard, died June 28, 1970. He was 74.

Elton Tabor died unexpectedly at the age of 57.

Maurice "Dude" Tabor died from a broken heart on August 13, 2007, six months after losing the love of his life, Margaret. He was 84.

Hutto Tabor was taken from us at the age of 45 as a result of a boating accident on Lake Claiborne, near Homer. He had with him at the time of the tragedy the following poem:

God grant that I might live to fish until my dying day,
And when my final cast I've made and life has slipped away,
I pray that God's great landing net will catch me in its sweep,
And in His mercy God will judge me big enough to keep.